Praise for
Scott Travers' Top 88 Coins to Buy & Sell

"The most important list of coin recommendations ever written."

—*COINage* magazine

"*Scott Travers' Top 88 Coins* is potentially enriching, educational and enlightening. It provides market-oriented information against a rich backdrop of the history and lore of coins. *Top 88* is far more than just an investment book—it's a landmark work that opens the world of coinage to the reader!"

—**R.W. Julian**
renowned numismatic scholar

"Follow the recommendations embodied in these pages, and you'll be well on the way to being a winner yourself!"

—**Ed Reiter**
former numismatics columnist,
the *New York Times*

{ **INVESTMENT BOOK OF THE YEAR WINNER**
from the Numismatic Literary Guild }

SCOTT TRAVERS'
TOP 88
COINS
TO BUY & SELL

SCOTT TRAVERS'
TOP 88 COINS
TO BUY & SELL
44 WINNERS AND 44 LOSERS

—— Second Edition ——

SCOTT A. TRAVERS

**HOUSE OF
COLLECTIBLES**

New York   Toronto   London   Sydney   Auckland

The author holds or has previously held positions in various for-profit and nonprofit hobby organizations. The views reflected in this book are his own and do not reflect the views of any such organization. The author also may have a financial or other interest in some or all of the products or organizations featured or reviewed in this book.

Coin photographs are for educational purposes and are not necessarily reproduced to scale.

All coin photographs are provided courtesy American Numismatic Rarities, LLC/Stack's Rarities, Wolfeboro, NH, except where indicated.

ON THE COVER:

Two winners and one loser on the cover: WINNER 1803 Draped Bust Heraldic Eagle gold piece grading Mint State-66 (top, center); WINNER 1856 Flying Eagle cent grading Proof-65; and LOSER 1925 Peace dollar grading Mint State-64. (*Photographs courtesy American Numismatic Rarities, LLC/Stack's Rarities, Wolfeboro, NH*)

Visit the House of Collectibles Web site: www.houseofcollectibles.com

Library of Congress Cataloging-in-Publication Data
Travers, Scott A.
    Scott Travers' top 88 coins to buy and sell : 44 winners and 44 losers / Scott A. Travers. — 2nd ed.
        p.   cm.
    ISBN 978-0-375-72221-9 (trade pbk. : alk. paper)   1. Coins, American—Collectors and collecting—Handbooks, manuals, etc.   2. Coins as an investment—Handbooks, manuals, etc.
I. Title.   II. Title: Top 88 coins to buy and sell.
    CJ1832.T74 2007
    332.63—dc22
                                                                                                            2007004429

Second Edition

Printed in the United States of America

10 9 8 7 6 5 4 3 2 1

CONTENTS

To my parents

ACKNOWLEDGMENTS

The author was assisted in preparing this book by a number of highly knowledgeable individuals who generously shared their expertise. Gratitude is extended to:

John Albanese, Ed Aleo, Gail Baker, Q. David Bowers, Candice Chaplin, Mike Chipman, Christopher Cipoletti, Aaron Cohodes, William L. Corsa, John W. Dannreuther, Beth Deisher, Thomas K. DeLorey, Richard Doty, Shane Downing, Michael R. Fuljenz, David L. Ganz, Salvatore Germano, Marcy Gibbel, Barbara Gregory, David Hall, James L. Halperin, Cary B. Hardy, David C. Harper, Sarri R. Harper, Dorothy F. Harris, Brian Hendelson, Alan Herbert, John Highfill, Erin Hughes, Jim Hughes, Robert L. Hughes, Steve Ivy, Robert W. Julian, Christine Karstedt, Melissa Karstedt, Charles H. Knull, Rahel Lerner, Kevin J. Lipton, Denis W. Loring, Lee S. Minshull, Tom Mulvaney, John Pack, Martin Paul, Donn Pearlman, Doug Plasencia, Larry Posner, Ed Reiter, Maurice H. Rosen, Deborah G. Rosenthal, Will Rossman, Mark Salzberg, Jeff Shoop, Rick Snow, Celeste Sollod, Larry Stack, Michael J. Standish, Sheryl Stebbins, Jeffrey A. Stern, David

Sundman, Anthony J. Swiatek, Barbara J. Travers, Harvey C. Travers, Michael White, Mark Yaffe, and Keith M. Zaner.

John Albanese, founder of the Numismatic Guaranty Corporation of America (NGC), provided extraordinary assistance in evaluating the winning and losing qualities of the coins presented. He selflessly drew upon his many years of experience as a world class coin trader and professional numismatist.

Rahel Lerner, editor for the Random House Information Group, drew upon her extraordinary intelligence and vast professional skills in editing the text, fine-tuning the manuscript, and helping to make the book a working reality. Her assistance in coordinating details from cover branding to image labeling was immensely important.

Ed Reiter rendered particularly valuable service in editing the text of the first edition, drawing upon his extensive background as a numismatic journalist, including nearly a decade as numismatics columnist of the *New York Times* and more than two decades as senior editor of *COINage* magazine.

American Numismatic Rarities, LLC/Stack's Rarities, Wolfeboro, NH, provided not only market insights, but also most of the photographs to accompany the text. Special thanks go to Doug Plasencia, the company's exceptionally talented photographer, for his work on these exceptional illustrations. And accolades also go to Christine Karstedt, the firm's president, for her diligent attention to detail on many aspects of this project.

The Smithsonian National Museum of American History/National Numismatic Collection made available digital images of two great rarities. Richard Doty, curator, and Jim Hughes, associate curator, were responsible for providing these courtesies.

INTRODUCTION

By Ed Reiter
Former numismatics columnist, the *New York Times*

Everyone loves a winner—and everyone loves to win.

Successful sports teams draw more fans than perennial also-rans. Best-selling authors get higher advances and bigger promotional budgets than struggling neophytes. Blue-chip stocks with proven track records attract more investors than marginal performers.

Football coach Vince Lombardi liked to say that winning isn't everything—it's the *only* thing. That absolutist approach may be better suited to professional athletics than to everyday life, but few would dispute that winning is better than losing. And that is surely true when it comes to buying rare coins—or, for that matter, *any* coins for which the seller charges you a premium.

COINS AND COLLECTING

Coin collecting is probably almost as old as coins themselves—and those date back more than two-and-a-half millennia, all the way to the seventh century B.C., when the first rudimentary coins appeared in the small Asia Minor kingdom of Lydia. Those earliest coins were crude pieces of gold and silver alloy stamped with a simple design—the head of a lion, for instance—to denote their official status.

For centuries, only men of wealth had the time and resources needed to pursue, procure, and preserve rare coins. Indeed, this came to be known as "The Hobby of Kings." As the modern era brought redistribution of wealth and greater leisure time for increasing numbers of people, coin collecting attracted an ever-growing army of recruits. Ironically, it enjoyed a period of major expansion during the Great Depression—a time when few people had any money to spare, much less save. Spurred by the introduction of inexpensive "coin boards," many Americans started devoting part of their newly enforced spare time to assembling sets of cents and other low-value coins from pocket change.

By the late 1950s, millions of Americans had extra cash to go with their extra time, and many began devoting substantial amounts of both to what had now become "The King of Hobbies." Since then, coin collecting has grown exponentially, to a degree few collectors would have imagined possible 50 years ago. No longer just a pleasant, diverting hobby pursued in people's living rooms or on their dining-room tables, it has become a dynamic, full-fledged industry in which coins are routinely sold for hundreds of thousands of dollars—and, with growing frequency, for millions.

WINNERS AND LOSERS

Vince Lombardi to the contrary, winning and losing aren't necessarily absolute. They can come in degrees and nuances, rather than being strictly black and white. Many times, for instance, a coin may be a winner at one price but a loser if you add, say, 20 percent—not so very much, really—to that price. Or a coin graded Mint State-64 may be a winner while its counterpart in Mint State-65—just one level higher on the 1-to-70 grading scale used throughout the marketplace—may be a loser. Today's winner could be tomorrow's loser if market conditions shift even moderately. Then again, some winners—and some losers—may retain those designations for the rest of their lives and ours.

There is one absolute winner associated with this book, and that is its author. Based on a professional and personal association dating back more than a quarter-century, I can vouch without reservation for the intelligence, independence, and integrity of Scott A. Travers. He is not only the most knowledgeable person I ever have encountered in the coin field, but also the most reputable. And unlike some experts I have encountered over the years, Scott willingly and enthusiastically shares his deep knowledge—not only through his books and magazine and newspaper articles, but also through frequent appearances at coin shows and other public forums, invariably at his own expense. Years ago, I described him in a *New York Times* column as "the Ralph Nader of numismatics," and this title is just as warranted now as it was the day I coined it. Scott watches over the interests of the little guy and, despite admonitions from those who fear adverse consequences for their own self-interest, he points out the perils and pitfalls year in and year out, steering the unwary away from the many traps that lurk in this complicated marketplace.

Scott Travers' Top 88 Coins to Buy & Sell is yet another service to the hobby, and especially to the little guy who needs help in steering clear of trouble. It isn't all-inclusive; no single book could possibly cover the subject comprehensively. But it highlights the things to look for—as well as the things to avoid. And while it doesn't color every nuance in vivid detail, it paints the broad outline so clearly and dramatically that readers cannot fail to get the picture.

Read this book closely and you'll get a new perspective on what really counts when you buy and sell coins. Follow the recommendations embodied in these pages and you'll be well on the way to being a winner yourself!

CHAPTER 1

INVESTING BIG MONEY IN SMALL CHANGE

Coins have been prized for centuries as collectibles, and those made of precious metal have long been treasured as stores of value. Not until modern times, however, have coins been widely pursued, in and of themselves, as an investment.

There were stirrings of such interest during the 1930s, when dozens of commemorative coins were issued by the U.S. Mint and large numbers of newcomers joined established collectors in setting them aside, drawn to a great extent by the hope and expectation that these coins would increase in value in years to come. Traditional collectors hadn't been oblivious to price appreciation prior to that time, but it wasn't what attracted most of them to coins. Their pursuit of these tiny treasures was motivated primarily by their fascination with the history, cultural significance, and aesthetic appeal embodied in these hand-held works of art, not by their hope of future gain.

The profit motive became an even stronger influence in the coin market in the 1950s, when a surge of speculative demand developed for newly issued U.S. proof sets—sets containing special, high-quality examples of current-year coins, issued each year by the U.S. Mint. Speculators then began buying up uncirculated rolls of late-date U.S. coins, reasoning that if one brand-new coin was a good thing, 50 must be 50 times as desirable. The roll boom crashed in the early 1960s, and interest in late-date proof sets waned, too.

One of the fundamental flaws of these early forms of coin investment was that they focused on coins that weren't really rare or even scarce. Modern U.S. coins frequently had mintages in the hundreds of millions. Even the 1955-S Lincoln cent, widely perceived as extremely scarce, had a mintage of more than 44.6 million. It made little sense, therefore, to pay $50 or more for a 50-cent roll of such a coin.

Ironically, truly scarce U.S. coins were ignored by many of the roll and proof-set buyers. These coins were increasing in value, but far less dramatically than their late-date, much more common counterparts. At the very time rolls of recent Lincoln cents and other modern coins were selling for big premiums over face value, 19th-century coins with mintages in the thousands carried modest price tags, as did genuinely scarce high-grade specimens of early 20th-century coins, such as "Mercury" dimes, Standing Liberty quarters, and Walking Liberty half dollars.

The Start of Something Big

By the early 1970s, a new breed of coin seller was evolving—one that saw the potential of scarce U.S. coins and realized they were being overlooked. Unlike traditional coin dealers, who tended to dress casually and deal with customers informally from behind display cases in shops, many of these new-style dealers wore business suits and conducted business in paneled offices, with most of their inventory locked away in safes. They dealt with clients, not collectors—and in truth, many of the buyers who visited their offices *weren't* hobbyists, but doctors, lawyers, and other businesspeople seeking a safe new haven for their money. In short, they were *investors*.

Before long, a two-tier marketplace developed, with one group of dealers serving primarily collectors and the other doing business with investors. In time, though, the two kinds of buyers moved closer together and found at least some areas of common ground.

Today, there is a coin buyers' spectrum. At one end is the collector, who buys coins for their artistic and cultural and historical significance. At the other end is the investor, who buys coins to go to the cash window and celebrate. Between these two ends of the spectrum is the collector/investor, a hybrid who is a combination of both. Some people are closer to being collectors than investors, and vice versa. The collector/investor understands how to get good value in the marketplace—how to buy coins without being ripped off—and also appreciates the beauty of coins and the artistic and cultural significance that they represent. When given an opportunity to realize a profit on a coin, a collector/investor might pause long enough to take a picture of it but then go and sell it and pocket the profit.

Coin investment got an enormous boost in 1974, when Congress passed legislation lifting the ban that for more than four decades had barred Americans from owning gold bullion. For the previous 40 years, only numismatic gold coins—those whose value as collectibles exceeded their face value—had been legal for Americans to own. When the ban officially ended on December 31, 1974, previously prohibited gold bullion coins, such as South Africa's

Krugerrand, poured into the fertile new U.S. market, and gold coins in general began to be marketed as investments on a level never before seen in this country. It was truly a monumental year for the coin marketplace.

Gold Coins as a Driving Market Force—Bullion Coins vs. Numismatic Coins

With the return of private gold ownership, collectors and investors had two ways of acquiring the lustrous yellow metal in coinage form: the numismatic coins with which they were already familiar, and which many already owned, and the newly legal bullion coins.

The Krugerrand dominated the bullion gold coin market at the time the ban was lifted, but in time it fell out of favor because of South Africa's apartheid policy and new competitors made major inroads. Among the most popular today are Canada's Maple Leaf and Uncle Sam's American Eagle. In 2006, a new American gold bullion coin—the one-ounce, 24-karat American Buffalo—arrived on the scene and became an immediate hit, largely because it bears virtually the same design as the much admired Buffalo nickel.

Typically, the value of a gold (or silver or platinum) bullion coin is based on the value of the metal it contains. The selling price usually reflects this bullion value plus a modest markup to cover the costs of production, distribution, and handling. Thus, when gold is worth $700 an ounce on the commodities market, a one-ounce bullion gold coin might cost $725 at a coin shop or other retail outlet.

A numismatic gold coin is partly a bullion investment; its gold content serves as a floor for its market value. But numismatic coins command additional premiums as collector's items, and their numismatic value can be many thousands of dollars, depending on their rarity and condition and the degree of demand for them. One numismatic gold coin—a 1933 double eagle (or $20 gold piece)—fetched $7.59 million at a 2002 auction sale in New York. That's the highest price ever paid at public auction for a single U.S. coin. (And yet, the coin is listed as a "loser" in this book! You'll soon see why.)

Bullion coins are sometimes perceived as having a numismatic component. China's Panda coins, for instance, have brought higher-than-usual premiums over the years because of their relatively low mintages and the popular appeal of their designs, which feature panda bears and are changed every year. Likewise, so-called "First Strike" Mint State-70 and Proof-70 examples of the American Buffalo were bringing thousands of dollars apiece soon after the coin's introduction because some buyers considered them rare in those high grades. I don't recommend paying such premiums; after all is said and done, bullion coins should be purchased at bullion-related prices.

If you're buying a gold bullion coin, you might pay a 5 percent markup over the dealer's cost of the coin, and if you're buying a rare gold coin, you might pay a 15, 20, 30, 40, or higher percent markup on the dealer's cost of the coin. Some gold bullion trades are subject to Internal Revenue Service 1099-B reporting, whereas gold collector coins are relatively private, not subject to 1099-B reporting. Gold bullion coins enjoy a wide market, while the rare-coin market is thinly capitalized.

Positive and Negative Influences

From 1975 through the end of the decade, the price of gold moved steadily higher as more and more Americans took the plunge and started buying gold in bullion (and bullion-coin) form. This, in turn, helped feed the parallel growth of interest—and price levels—in the rare-coin market. It provided early evidence that strength in precious metals usually is accompanied by similar strength in collectible coins.

The basic appeal of gold is that it has been a timeless store of value through the ages. Gold is calamity insurance against an uncertain world. When the dollar is weak, gold grows stronger. In the mid-1970s, when gold began its climb, it was selling for less than $200 an ounce. The big question today is whether gold is going to hit $1,000 an ounce. It might be at that level by the time you read this—or it might be lower. Gold coins have been viewed for centuries as a safe haven in times of economic calamity and political turmoil, and today, they are seen by many as a way to safeguard at least a portion of one's wealth against the ominous threat of global terrorism. Gold coins are a harbor of protection—and a safe harbor, at that. When there's blood in the streets, millions of people turn to the gold under their mattresses.

Precious-metal prices are among a number of economic factors that affect demand for coins as an investment.

Traditionally, inflation in the nation's money supply has had a highly positive impact on the investment coin market. That's because rare coins, like precious metals, have always been viewed as an inflationary hedge. Thus, when inflation is high, there's economic and psychological impetus to buy hard assets and keep them under the mattress, figuratively and sometimes literally, as protection in case things get even worse. In 1979 and 1980, the last two full years of Jimmy Carter's presidency, rampant inflation played a major role in triggering the greatest boom the rare-coin market has ever known.

Deflation, on the other hand, is bad for coin investment. When money is tight and people feel a financial pinch, there's less disposable income to spend on discretionary items such as coins and precious metals—and less inclination to spend it that way. Let's say you bought a house for $250,000 and it went up in value to $1 million. You'd be favorably disposed toward spending $50,000 of your increased net worth for rare coins. But if you bought a house for $1 million and its value fell to $250,000, you'd feel a lot less comfortable investing your diminished wealth in small metallic trinkets. That's the effect of deflation: It makes you feel poorer and far less inclined to part with your money.

People invest in coins when they see what newsletter writer Maurice Rosen refers to as "economic justification" for coin prices to go higher. When bullion prices are rising, they feel comfortable and confident entering the rare coin marketplace. When the bullion market is weak, they tend to steer clear of rare coins. In times of economic prosperity, coins increase in value. And in times of depression or recession, coins are laggard and don't do very well.

Going for the Gold

Increasing numbers of American consumers are buying gold—and pushing up its price; the gold rush is being driven by widespread uneasiness over the U.S. government's political and economic policies.

This heightened anxiety over the nation's political and economic problems should send the price of gold—and especially rare gold coins—much higher in the years ahead. Some leading analysts are forecasting $3,000 per ounce gold by 2010. When gold was $400 per ounce, I was telling attendees at my seminars held at coin conventions that I expected $700 an ounce gold in 2006. Gold hit that milestone, as I predicted.

The fear of domestic inflation, an eroding dollar, higher oil prices, terrorist attacks, a high deficit, and the potential for financial chaos combine to make gold more attractive than ever before.

The price of gold bullion has more than doubled in the last five years, from $248 an ounce in 2001 to $587 in October 2006. And collectible gold coins have done even better in many cases, increasing in value several hundred percent in just the last two years. For instance, a lightly circulated 1799 ten-dollar gold piece has tripled in value from $10,000 in 2004 to $30,000 today, and similar examples abound.

At a time when even a modest rise in the price of gasoline draws immediate attention nationwide, gold's remarkable jump in value has gone largely unnoticed by most Americans. It has taken place "under the radar screen." Collectible gold coins are a stealth commodity. Because of their special nature, their audience is relatively small. But they have been doing extremely well, and despite the large gains already made, they still represent an excellent buying opportunity. In terms of their real value, they remain cheap.

In 1980, the national debt was $1 trillion and the total U.S. money supply was less than $2 trillion when gold hit its all-time high of $887.50 an ounce. Today, with gold at less than two-thirds its 1980 peak, the national debt is $8 trillion and the money supply exceeds

$10 trillion. Thus, gold is still undervalued despite having doubled in price since 2001.

I see the sharp rise in gold's value as resulting directly from government policies and the American public's concern about those policies.

We have become a debtor nation. In the 1980s, we were a creditor nation and gold was generally stable—even stagnant—as Americans grew confident about the economy. Today, we need $2 billion a day from foreign countries to make up for our $68.5 billion-a-month trade deficit. We are building a massive amount of debt that has to be paid.

Coin Investing's Three Basic Risks

If you plan to go out and buy some of the 44 "winners" described in this book, or any coins, for that matter, you need to be aware of three major risks that could bear on your investment.

The first is the acquisition risk—the risk that you may pay too much at the time of purchase. If you pay $1,000 for a coin you buy at a flea market, there's a good chance that it may be worth a lot less, possibly only $100. Likewise, if you buy that coin from a dealer who isn't reputable, you can easily get burned. You should patronize dealers who are members of the American Numismatic Association, the national coin club, or the Professional Numismatists Guild, a prestigious, dealers-only organization. Both of these organizations police unethical practices by their members and provide procedures for resolving disputes when they arise. The acquisition risk is a significant one, because no matter how good the market is, or how reputable the seller is when you buy a coin, if you overpay upfront you may never be able to recover. You can minimize the acquisition risk by doing business with reputable dealers and educating yourself to the ways of the marketplace. Two of my other books, *One-Minute Coin Expert* and *The Coin Collector's Survival Manual*, will help you overcome acquisition risks.

The second major risk is the market risk—the risk that if you buy a coin for $1,000, it can plummet in value to $100 after you purchase it. You can limit the market risk by reading up on coin values, boning up on the coin market, studying market cycles, and understanding the relationship between gold and silver bullion and the rare-coin marketplace.

The third risk is the sale risk—the risk that if you buy a coin for $1,000 and it increases in value to $10,000, you may run afoul of a disreputable dealer when the time comes to sell that coin, or end up back in that flea market. Then, instead of getting $10,000, you could be offered a great deal less. Knowledge is the key to reducing this risk or eliminating it altogether. The more you know about coins and about the marketplace, the less likely it is that you'll be ripped off. Instead, you'll laugh in the face of that disreputable dealer when he offers to buy that $10,000 coin for just $500.

These are three very serious risks, and none of them should be underestimated when you invest in coins.

Coin Grading

Up until the late 1970s, the process by which coins were graded—or rated on their level of preservation—was arbitrary, vague, and subjective. Each dealer had his or her own system for determining the condition of a coin, and the terminology used to express that condition tended to consist of imprecise adjectives such as "gem," "choice," "typical," and even "nice." That approach was adequate at a time when coin prices didn't increase dramatically from one level of preservation to the next-highest level. But as prices began to surge and greater stress was placed on the quality of rare coins, resulting in much steeper price gains for new (or "uncirculated") coins, the need for a better system became apparent.

The American Numismatic Association took the lead in developing grading standards, which it published in 1977, and expanded the role of the ANA Certification Service (ANACS) in 1979 to include not only authentication (something it had been doing since 1972) but also grading.

In place of strictly adjectival descriptions, ANA chose a numerical scale in order to convey a sense of greater precision. It did so by adapting the 1-to-70 scale introduced decades earlier by Dr. William Sheldon, a specialist in U.S. large cents, to reflect the relative values of coins in that Early American series. In the ANA system, 1 denotes a coin in poor condition, while 70 represents perfection—a mint-fresh coin devoid of flaws or blemishes. A "Mint State" range from 60 to 70 was reserved for uncirculated coins.

Initially, the ANA had a virtual monopoly on coin grading. But the field was revolutionized in 1986 when a group of professional numismatists headed by California coin dealer David Hall formed a new grading service with a much stronger market orientation: the Professional Coin Grading Service (PCGS). Coins submitted to this new company would be graded by three experienced coin sellers, with their grades being determined by taking a consensus of their independent opinions. "Consensus grading" was among a number of important PCGS innovations. It also introduced what came to be

1879 Coiled Hair "Stella" $4 gold piece. This exceptionally rare high-grade coin, sold for under $400,000 in 2002, is now worth more than double its purchase price. The coin was certified and graded by the Professional Coin Grading Service.

Photo courtesy Scott Travers Rare Coin Galleries, LLC

known as "slabbing": After grading coins, it encapsulated them in sonically sealed, tamper-resistant hard plastic holders. These provided a high degree of security—and by sealing a coded tab designating the grade in the same protective holder, PCGS eliminated the possibility that coins might be replaced by less valuable ones after grading.

Imitation being the sincerest form of flattery, a major competitor—the Numismatic Guaranty Corporation of America (NGC)—opened for business in 1987. In the years that followed, other grading services also have appeared on the scene, including the Independent Coin Grading Co. (ICG) and a new version of ANACS, which has been privately owned since the ANA sold it in 1990.

I strongly recommend that you limit your purchases of investment-quality coins to those that have been certified and encapsulated by one of the leading grading services. These enjoy ready acceptance in the marketplace, often trading on a sight-unseen basis because most buyers and sellers are confident that their grades are accurate. By contrast, "raw" or uncertified coins trade at a discount because of

Photo courtesy Scott Travers Rare Coin Galleries, LLC

1806 KNOBBED 6 $5
MS 64
2030766-006
NUMISMATIC GUARANTY CORPORATION

1806 Knobbed 6, 7 X6 Stars, Capped Bust Heraldic Eagle $5 gold piece. Feverish demand persists for this perennial winning coin type and top market performer. It carries a value of over $60,000. The coin was certified and graded by the Numismatic Guaranty Corporation of America.

uncertainty regarding the grades the services would assign to them if they were submitted for certification. Unless otherwise noted, all of the grades discussed in this book are those assigned by either PCGS or NGC. In addition to being the largest, these services have greater market acceptance than their competitors.

Be wary of dealers who certify their own coins—a practice I refer to "self-certification." And if you have coins in your attic, get them certified by a reputable service. It's the surest way to maximize their value.

How Coins Are Graded—on a Scale of 1 through 70

The definitions here refer strictly to business-strike coins, or those produced for use in commerce, although the use of the numbers has been extended to proofs, as well. Any coin in the Mint State category should possess no wear. Nonetheless, remember always to carefully inspect a coin's highest points, no matter how high a grade it is purported to be in.

Mint State-70. A Mint State-70 coin must be absolutely perfect in every respect.

An MS-70 must have full, radiant, dynamic luster; dramatic, breathtaking, and universally beautiful eye appeal; and no imperfections or flaws whatsoever (that includes the entire coin: obverse, reverse, edge, and rims).

Coins in the perfect classification must be fully struck, because anything less than a full strike would cause a coin to have less-than-perfect aesthetic appeal.

Coins classified as MS-70 cannot possess any Mint-made imperfections. These, too, would cause the coin to have less-than-perfect aesthetic appeal.

Mint State-69. The MS-69 designation is reserved for perfection's-threshold examples of the first magnitude.

Coins graded MS-69 must have no visible imperfections on either obverse or reverse under a 10-power glass. However, under higher-power magnification, some flaws might become obvious. Under 10-power magnification, one or two nearly imperceptible rim flaws might be visible.

The MS-69 designation can be used only if the coin has full and vibrant luster and, in general, if it has all the characteristics of the MS-70, with the exceptions mentioned.

Mint State-68. A coin graded MS-68 must appear perfect under 10-power magnification, with the exception of a nearly imperceptible scratch, nick, or flaw that appears in a non-grade-sensitive area (e.g., the hair).

Upon first glance, an MS-68 will appear to be perfect, and even some experts may have trouble finding the imperfection.

The MS-68, like the MS-69, may show some nearly imperceptible rim flaws under a 10-power glass.

The overall eye-appeal must be dramatic and awe-inspiring.

Mint State-67. An MS-67 is a wonder coin that you need not wonder about. Its luster, strike, and meticulously preserved surfaces make it exceptional. Intense luster usually emanates from immaculate surfaces.

There may be a detraction or two visible with a 5-power glass. MS-67 examples are truly elusive coins. Even though coins graded MS-68 and MS-69 exist, you really can't expect better than MS-67.

Mint State-66. An MS-66 coin is in the same high level of preservation as its MS-65 counterpart, but possesses some unusually superior or MS-67 characteristic.

A coin that has the surfaces of an MS-67, but has the Mint luster of an MS-65 might be deserving of the MS-66 grade.

Mint State-65. MS-65 is an important benchmark grade, as it is the minimum grade for a "gem." An MS-65 or gem coin cannot be lackluster or weakly struck. If either of these characteristics exists, the marketplace has dictated that a downgrading to 64 be considered.

An MS-65 cannot have excessive nicks, scratches, marks, or flaws of any kind. But it is by no means a perfect coin. There is room for minor detractions visible with a 5-power glass.

An MS-65 should have an overall pleasing appearance, free from marks and rich with luster and detail.

Mint State-64. A cursory glance at a coin deserving this grade would indicate that a grade of MS-65 is in order.

But close inspection of an MS-64 coin reveals a detracting overall characteristic, such as the lack of full Mint bloom or an excess of surface marks.

What sets the MS-64 coin apart from its MS-63 counterpart is its nearly convincing claim to MS-65 grading.

The grade of MS-64 has become an important marketplace grade. The market has determined that if an MS-65 example of a certain coin is valued at, say, $10,000, but its MS-63 counterpart is worth only $500, then a specimen valued at $3,000 has to be graded MS-64.

An MS-64 coin can be lightly fingerprinted or can exhibit weakness of strike in important areas.

An MS-64 coin is indisputably better than an MS-63 but not deserving of the MS-65 grade and, usually, the accompanying high MS-65 price.

Mint State-63. An MS-63 coin will often have claims to 65, except for the presence of noticeable marks visible to the unaided eye.

An MS-63 may have toning that is not universally appealing and may be nearly fully struck, but, perhaps, not 100 percent fully struck.

MS-63s are often found with fingerprints whose darkening is of varying degrees.

Copper and nickel coins graded MS-63 will often be spotted with dark toning areas that penetrate the surface of the coin. If these spots are deemed too detracting, a downgrading to MS-62 may be necessary.

INVESTING BIG MONEY IN SMALL CHANGE

Mint State-62. An MS-62 coin is an above-average Mint State example. It is a coin that does not overwhelm the viewer with scratches, abrasions, and other detractions.

Coins in this category possess all of the characteristics of their 63 counterparts, except that they are deficient—but only slightly—in quality of surface or Mint bloom.

Mint State-61. An MS-61 coin must have no wear on its highest points. It must not have been circulated.

Scratches, abrasions, and other imperfections will appear on coins of this classification.

The primary distinction of the MS-61 that separates it from its MS-60 counterpart is the 61's lack of a primary detracting gash or other imperfection in a grade-sensitive area.

Although the MS-61 may have numerous and multiple marks, imperfections, and other flaws, none will be of such a magnitude that it will become a primary focus of the coin. The MS-61 will not nearly qualify for the status of "damaged."

An MS-61 can be lackluster or dull as well as have unattractive toning.

Mint State-60. An MS-60 coin must have no wear on its highest points. It must not have been circulated.

The MS-60 example will fall just short of being classified as a damaged coin.

Scratches, abrasions, imperfections visible to the unaided eye, and major detractions will characterize coins of this grade.

Large coins, such as silver dollars and double eagles ($20 gold pieces), will have, in addition to the multiplicity of scratches and nicks, at least one major gash, flaw, or other imperfection in a grade-sensitive area (e.g., Ms. Liberty's cheek on the Morgan dollar).

Copper and nickel coins of this grade, in addition to the surface imperfections, may have problems of corrosive porosity that deeply penetrate the surface.

An MS-60 can be lackluster or dull, as well as have unattractive toning.

Occasionally, an MS-60 will be found without that one particularly detracting flaw, but the coin will possess multiple flaws, pits, and deep scratches.

About Uncirculated-58. An AU-58 coin must appear Mint State at first glance.

Upon close examination, light friction will be visible on the highest points. (Imagine a perspiration-soaked thumb rubbing the coin, and envision the aftermath.)

An AU-58 ordinarily would qualify for the MS-63 grade. However, the light rubbing would remove it from technically being classified as "Mint State."

Sometimes, AU-58 coins trade among dealers at the MS-63 price (or close to it) because of the overall aesthetic quality of the coin.

Coins graded below AU-58 generally trade for substantially lower prices than those graded AU-58 and above. That's because high quality is deemed to be an important determinant of value, along with low mintage and high demand. The lower the numerical value assigned to a given coin, the lower its grade (or level of preservation).

And the lower the grade, the more imperfections a coin is likely to have—including heavy wear, obvious nicks and scratches, and dull-looking surfaces.

The lowest recognized grade, Poor-1, denotes a coin so heavily worn and possibly banged up that someone examining it has to look closely to tell what kind of coin it is and what its date is—two minimum criteria for grading a coin at all. All numbers from 1 to 58 correspond to circulated coins—those that have seen actual use in commerce. But those graded AU-58 frequently are traded on the same financial par with Mint State coins because they are so close in appearance.

Below AU-58, the generally recognized grades in the circulated range are as follows, from highest to lowest:

- **About Uncirculated-55**
- **About Uncirculated-50**
- **Extremely Fine-45**
- **Extremely Fine-40**
- **Very Fine-30**
- **Very Fine-20**
- **Fine-12**
- **Very Good-8**
- **Good-4**
- **About Good-3**
- **Poor-1**

This is the lowest grade. A coin grading 1 is so well worn and has passed through so many hands that it is barely identifiable as to its type.

The Elements of Grading

What factors determine the grade of a coin? There are several:

- **The strike**

  Is the coin well struck or is it weakly struck? Does it contain all of the elements intended by its designer? Strike is the degree of design detail present on a coin at the time it is minted.

- **The eye appeal**

  Is it pretty or ugly? Does it look unattractive or does it grab your attention with its pleasing appearance? Does it have beautiful concentric-circle toning? Blazing, satinlike luster? Or is it dark and ugly?

  The three basic components of eye appeal are luster, toning, and surfaces.

- *Luster*

  Is the coin lackluster? Has it been "dipped" too much—left too long in a mildly acidic solution to remove detracting coloring from its surface? Luster is the quality of a coin's light reflective properties.

- *Toning*

  Does it have visible spots? Is it unnaturally toned? Toning is the slow, natural process by which a coin darkens in color over a period of months and years.

- *Surfaces*

  Has the coin been cleaned? The telltale sign of cleaning is if a coin has crisscrossing parallel striations, or light, almost imperceptible hairline scratches.

- **Environmental damage**

  If a coin has been damaged by the environment, the leading grading services will return the coin ungraded. One of the leading causes of coins being returned is damage from polyvinyl chloride plasticizers seeping out from degrading soft plastic holders onto the surfaces of the coins.

Rare-coin Value Keys

Understanding what makes a coin a winner or a loser has much to do with three basic rare-coin value keys.

The first value key is the grade. A coin that looks as if Godzilla used it as a teething ring is clearly less desirable than another coin that looks pristine and new, as if it were minted just yesterday, with no imperfections and no flaws. The fewer flaws a coin has, the more desirable it is and the higher its price will be.

The second factor is the supply—how many examples have been minted and how many of those still exist. The lower the available supply, the higher the price is likely to be.

The third factor is the demand. If there are just 10 examples of a certain coin available but only nine people want them, the value of those coins won't be nearly as high as the small supply might suggest. You can have a coin that's nearly perfect and that's relatively scarce, but if the demand doesn't exceed the supply, it's not going to have a very high value.

Mastering these three basic concepts will help you to decide on your own whether a coin is a winner or a loser. But keep in mind, a coin can go from one column to the other—from winner to loser, and vice versa—almost overnight. In fact, in the 10 years since the first edition of this book was published, some of the coins I selected *have* gone from one column to the next overnight. So between editions, you have a responsibility to yourself to understand and apply these three rare-coin value keys so you can determine whether the coin you're buying today is a winner or a loser, irrespective of what you read in my book or anyone else's book.

Registry Sets

To stimulate interest in its services, PCGS now offers what it calls a Set Registry™ program. Under this program, collectors who own coins certified by PCGS arrange those coins into sets and "register" the sets by entering the coins' PCGS serial numbers on the company's Web site. Using special software, PCGS then assigns ratings to these sets reflecting the rarity of the coins and the grades in which they were certified, plus or minus points for the presence or absence of unusual characteristics (such as "full heads" on Standing Liberty quarters). It determines the overall rating of a set by a mathematical formula, then lists all sets sequentially on the Web site, from the highest rating down. The top-rated sets, judged in various categories, are singled out for special recognition. NGC offers a similar registry program, but accepts not only NGC-graded coins but also those in PCGS holders.

The registry programs have proved extremely popular; their competitive nature stimulates a "Can you top this?" attitude among many collectors. In their effort to achieve high rankings and gain recognition, however, some collectors get carried away and pay exorbitant sums for coins with exceptionally high grades. This poses the risk of serious financial loss, especially in the case of pristine modern coins such as common-date Lincoln cents and Jefferson nickels. There have been instances where overzealous registry set collectors have paid $25,000, $30,000, or $40,000 for a coin that might be worth only 40 cents under normal circumstances and in a slightly lower level of preservation.

Being a Big Winner

There's big money in small coins, and this book will serve as your action plan for ferreting out the coins that can bring you that big money, and then make that big money even bigger.

The "winners" and "losers" in this book include some coins worth millions of dollars apiece and others worth only modest premiums (or even no premium at all, in the case of certain "losers"). There is literally something for everyone. And while you might not be able to afford to own the million-dollar rarities, you can learn a great deal by studying the factors that make them so desirable—and, by applying those lessons, become a savvier buyer when buying coins that do fit your budget. You'll learn—surprise!—that even a coin costing millions can be classified as a loser under certain market conditions.

Read my recommendations carefully, but then do your homework. And apply the lessons you learn.

Do business with reputable dealers. Learn how the marketplace operates. Become a collector/investor—one who seeks financial appreciation but also appreciates the artistic, cultural, and historical significance of coins. Study the series you're buying, but also weigh the financial implications of your purchases. Know a coin's value and its current grading standards at all times. That's extremely important. Know what your coins are worth and don't get ripped off. Limit yourself to coins that have been certified by the leading grading services. Grading standards have changed over time and they may continue to change, so you need to educate yourself. Go to conventions, go to seminars, attend ANA conventions. Read books. Stay informed. That's clearly a very basic caveat.

Be decisive and take action. If you bought a coin for $500 and it goes up in value to $5,000, don't sit on your hands—sell that coin. Get rid of your underperformers and your junk. You'll read about such "losers" in this book, and you should start selling them immediately.

Do all this and you're sure to be a winner yourself—even if the coins you buy don't always fall under that heading.

CHAPTER 2

THE TOP 88 COINS

WINNER
1

Common-date Saint-Gaudens double eagles graded Mint State-65

Not so many years ago, common-date Saint-Gaudens double eagles would have been considered losers in the highly desirable grade of Mint State-65. It's not that the coins were unattractive; on the contrary, they bear a design of exceptional beauty created by Augustus Saint-Gaudens, considered by many the finest American sculptor of his day. And in gem condition, the level to which MS-65 corresponds, their majesty can be seen in its full glory on every coin in the series, which spanned the period from 1907 to 1933. The problem was, many prospective buyers were reluctant to pay big premiums for coins with relatively high mintages—however magnificent their design and however dazzling their appearance. As a result, these coins were lackluster performers in the marketplace.

Times have changed considerably, however. The surging price of gold in recent years has stimulated enormous investor interest in precious metals. This has swept away the caution that made many buyers reluctant to pay extra for common-date gold coins, no matter what their condition. And as they have opened their billfolds and checkbooks to purchase such coins in growing numbers, the coins' premium value has risen dramatically.

The price gains are fully justified, for "Saints," as these $20 gold pieces are affectionately known throughout the hobby, have much to offer. Their portraits are widely regarded as the most aesthetically stunning ever to appear on U.S. coinage, with a striding figure of Liberty on the obverse and a soaring American eagle on the reverse. In higher grades, including MS-65, their beauty is particularly breathtaking, showcased, as it is, with a minimum of flaws and a maximum of luster and detail. Truly, these mark the apex of U.S. coinage artistry. And each contains nearly an ounce of gold, reinforcing their numismatic appeal with a solid underpinning of high intrinsic value.

Precisely because they *are* so desirable and have such a high gold content, common-date Saints graded MS-65 have been hyped extensively as a solid investment vehicle for well-heeled buyers outside the hobby. Many of them have bought these coins, which has proved to be a mixed blessing for the coin market. Possessing only superficial knowledge about investment coins and lacking a sense of involvement with the hobby, these buyers have been fickle, abandoning their holdings at the first sign of coin-market weakness. Largely for this reason, demand for high-grade Saints was highly unpredictable in the face of plunging or stagnant gold prices. At the same time, there has been a dramatic increase in the available supply as more and more coins have been certified by the third-party grading services. As of October 2006, the Professional Coin Grading Service and the Numismatic Guaranty Corporation of America had certified a combined total of 24,059 Saints as MS-65.

But at this writing, Saints are enjoying an upward market cycle and currently are bringing $2,000 in MS-65. That's a fair price for coins that were selling for $5,000 each in 1988. Be careful, though: Saints are subject to sharp declines in demand and major increases in supply. And if gold declines in value significantly from its current level of $600 an ounce, these coins could well slide back into the loser column.

High-grade Saints are truly spectacular coins, and their current price is right—if the coins are carefully selected to be premium-quality specimens and as free from flaws as possible. Here's a case where beautiful coins might very well be beautiful investments too.

Photograph courtesy the Smithsonian National Museum of American History/National Numismatic Collection

The 1933 Saint-Gaudens double eagle

The 1933 double eagle ($20 gold piece) would seem to be a winner in anyone's book. The only specimen legally in private hands as this is written, in October 2006, brought $7.59 million when it was sold at auction in July 2002. That's the highest price ever paid for a single coin at public auction—nearly twice as much as the previous record-holder.

Since then, however, 10 more examples of the coin have come to light. And although the U.S. Mint has effectively confiscated them, legal proceedings now under way are challenging that seizure and possibly clearing the way for the coins to enter the marketplace. If that happens, the value of each 1933 Saint—including the one that brought $7.59 million—will surely be much less than that record sum, at least initially.

Beyond that, there are strong indications that even more 1933 double eagles are being held clandestinely by coin dealers, collectors, and other private individuals, probably including some overseas, where Uncle Sam cannot reach them.

Given the uncertainty about the future availability of the 10 coins now being held by the government, and possibly still more currently in hiding, I can't declare the '33 Saint a winner. There's simply too much uncertainty about how many examples might be available to collectors once the legal dust settles. Depending on how many come onto the market, they certainly could still be worth a million dollars each, maybe several million. And from that point on, all should enjoy steady and substantial appreciation. In short, they could then be big winners. But for now, the single coin that's legal to own must be considered a loser.

The 1933 double eagle wasn't born rare; it had a healthy mintage of 445,500. But before the Mint could release them, President Franklin D. Roosevelt issued his Gold Surrender Order halting further production of gold coins and recalling those held by private citizens (except for coins of numismatic value). Virtually the entire mintage of '33 Saints went into the melting pot. But "virtually" isn't "absolutely."

Within a few years, examples of the coin began turning up in the hands of dealers and collectors. The Mint did nothing at first, but in 1944, alerted to an auction including a '33 Saint, it decided the coin was illegal to own and sent the Secret Service to seize it. Other such seizures followed, and for decades hobbyists viewed all 1933 double eagles as being forbidden fruit, subject to confiscation by Uncle Sam.

The government's rationale was—and is—that the coins are illegal to own because they were never legal in the first place, never having been issued to the public. In recent years, however, numismatic experts have questioned that claim more aggressively, arguing that some of the coins may indeed have left the Mint in legitimate fashion. The matter came to a head after a '33 Saint said to have belonged to Egypt's King Farouk was seized from a dealer in 1996 in a Secret Service sting operation in New York.

Faced with a court test of its longstanding claim of illegality, the Mint reached a settlement with the dealer: It would declare this specimen—and only this specimen—legal to own and permit the dealer to sell it at auction, provided that he split the proceeds 50-50 with the government. It did so on the basis that a U.S. export license had been issued for the coin in 1944 permitting its conveyance to King Farouk, and that this conferred legitimacy upon it.

In many observers' eyes, the Mint went out of its way to avoid a showdown then, and doesn't want one now, because its arguments are shaky and could easily be rejected by a judge.

The 1933 double eagle has become a numismatic icon, much like the 1804 silver dollar and the 1913 Liberty Head nickel. Its headline-making history only heightens its appeal. But until the present uncertainty is dispelled, I have no choice but to list it as a loser.

Lafayette dollars graded Mint State-65

France played a pivotal role in helping the American colonists win their independence from Great Britain, and no single Frenchman was more crucial in that effort than the Marquis de Lafayette. France had not yet entered the American Revolution when the wealthy young nobleman, then just 19 years old, sailed to Philadelphia in 1777 to join the colonial army. Quickly gaining the confidence of Gen. George Washington, he was appointed a major general and fought with distinction through the end of the war, despite being wounded in the Battle of Brandywine.

In 1899, on the eve of the 1900 World's Fair in Paris, American admirers came up with the idea of erecting a statue in Lafayette's honor in Paris as a gift to France from the people of America. To help raise funds for the project, the Lafayette Memorial Commission petitioned Congress to authorize production of 100,000 commemorative half dollars, which it then could sell at a premium. Congress instead authorized 50,000 silver dollars, which were offered for sale for $2 each.

The Lafayette dollar is a fascinating coin. It was the first U.S. commemorative silver dollar and the only one from the "traditional" period of U.S. commemorative coinage. It was the first legal-tender U.S. coin to portray a real American (George Washington, who is shown in profile along with Lafayette). And though it is dated 1900, its entire mintage was produced on a single day, Dec. 14, 1899—the 100th anniversary of Washington's death. Only 36,000 examples of the coin were distributed (the rest were melted years later), and many of these saw circulation. As a result, relatively few examples exist in mint condition, making this a scarce and coveted rarity with a strong collector base. I especially recommend it in Mint State-65, a grade in which this coin is aesthetically pleasing and eminently collectible. It is priced at about $11,000 in this grade. The combined NGC and PCGS population figures for this coin in MS-65 are about 400 pieces.

Iowa commemorative half dollars graded Mint State-65

Commemorative coinage, like proof coins and other frills, spent World War II on the sidelines while the U.S. Mint focused all its efforts on meeting the demand for coinage of the realm. The commemorative coin program was suspended in 1939 and didn't resume until 1946, when Congress authorized a special half dollar to celebrate the centennial of Iowa's admission to the Union. It turned out to be one of only three new commemorative coins in the traditional section of the series issued after World War II.

The Iowa half dollar wasn't the highest-mintage coin from the so-called traditional period of U.S. commemoratives, which stretched from 1892 to 1954. A number of other issues had higher production figures than this coin's 100,000. But unlike many of those others, the Iowa's net population wasn't reduced by large-scale melting; no unsold coins were returned to the Mint, so all 100,000 (or virtually all, at least) remained available. Furthermore, Iowa halves tend to be sharply struck and problem-free, so many have been certified as Mint State-65. As of October 2006, the Professional Coin Grading Service and the Numismatic Guaranty Corporation of America had certified a combined total of more than 10,000 Iowa half dollars—4,335 of them as Mint State-65.

What worries some observers isn't that so many Iowa halves have been "slabbed" by the grading services, but rather that so many more *remain* to be certified. Approximately 85 percent of the total mintage hasn't been submitted to the certifiers yet, and this serves as a huge overhang—and a potentially serious depressant on the current market value of about $300 in Mint State-65. There's a lot of corn in Iowa—and a lot of Iowa coins.

Trade dollars graded Proof-64, 65, 66, or 67

In 1873, Congress passed far-reaching legislation that had a profound effect on U.S. coinage. Among other things, the legislation authorized a new silver coin slightly heavier than the standard silver dollar and containing slightly more precious metal. This coin, called the Trade dollar, was meant to give U.S. businessmen an advantage in their dealings with merchants in the Orient, especially the Chinese.

Besides producing this coin in a business-strike version for use in overseas trade, the U.S. Mint also made small quantities of proofs every year for sale to the nation's collectors. These sales were quite modest, given that relatively few Americans collected coins in earnest at that time. In the 13-year history of the Trade dollar, the number of proofs exceeded 1,000 in only four years.

This odd silver coin never really achieved its objective as a vehicle for international trade, and after just six years its production for that purpose was suspended. The Mint continued to issue proof specimens, though, from 1879 to 1885 before retiring the coin altogether.

In the final two years, the numbers it made were minuscule: 10 in 1884 and a mere 5 in 1885. These, of course, are great rarities and command enormous premiums, putting them beyond the reach of the typical coin buyer. The other Trade dollar proofs are far more available and affordable, but nonetheless qualify as legitimately rare coins, with mintages ranging from a low of 510 in 1877 to a high of 1,987 in 1880. Considering how elusive they are, they represent good values at current market levels—about $4,200 in Proof-64, $10,000 in Proof-65, $12,000 in Proof-66, and $20,000 in Proof-67. They are rare, beautiful, old, historic, and desirable.

A complete set of Eisenhower dollars, proof and uncirculated, in typical Mint State condition

As of this writing, some dealers are advertising complete sets of Eisenhower dollars for not much more than $250. These sets include all the proofs, plus all the business-strike pieces in mint condition. This sounds like a pretty good deal; even though this series lasted just eight years, you're getting more than two dozen coins, they're all brand new, and some of them contain precious metal (a reduced silver content of 40 percent). Actually, it isn't the worst deal in the world. But it's also far from the best, for the Eisenhower dollars found in most such sets are commonplace and unlikely to appreciate significantly in value.

Although they are extremely scarce and potentially quite valuable in very high levels of preservation, Eisenhower dollars are readily available—and worth little or nothing above face value—in typical uncirculated condition. Hundreds of millions were minted, and many of these, while technically uncirculated, are aesthetically unappealing. They're weakly struck, bag-marked, lacking in luster, and, all in all, rather ugly. These are the kinds of coins that often end up in ready-made sets. Ike dollars also are common in proof, and while a Mint State-67 piece could be worth a pretty penny, a Proof-67 example probably would bring only a nominal premium. The bottom line is, you're paying $100·or more for coins that are available by the millions in a set that has minimal intrinsic value and almost no potential to rise in value as a collectible.

Rather than spending $250 for an entire set of common Ike dollars, you'd be better off spending a little more and getting a single coin in Mint State-66. That's where the potential for future gain exists. Remember, though, that the earlier dates are scarcest in pristine mint condition, and the coins to buy are the business strikes, not the proofs.

The 1804 silver dollar

The 1804 silver dollar is one of the most famous U.S. coins and one of the most valuable. The finest-known example changed hands at public auction in August 1999 for $4.14 million, and for nearly three years, that held the record as the highest price ever paid for a single coin at public auction. The previous record-holder? A different 1804 silver dollar, which brought $1.84 million at an auction in 1997.

The 1804 dollar isn't the rarest U.S. coin. Fifteen examples are known, and a number of other coins exist in smaller quantities, even to the point of being unique. But few if any U.S. coins possess the historic appeal and romantic allure that make this silver dollar so endlessly intriguing to collectors. It's a winner in every way, and although few can realistically hope to own it, everyone can admire it from afar and derive vicarious pleasure from its fascinating story.

Part of the lure of the 1804 dollar stems from its long status as a coin of mystery. Examples of the coin didn't start turning up until the mid-1800s, even though U.S. Mint records stated that 19,570 silver dollars had been struck in 1804. Even then, there were few sightings, and as time went by, many collectors assumed that most of the coins listed by the Mint had been melted, making the surviving specimens rare.

This theory persisted for more than a century until, at last, in 1962, researchers Eric Newman and Kenneth E. Bressett came up with what now is accepted as the real explanation. The key to their theory was the emergence of the so-called King of Siam Proof Set, which had been in the possession of a British family, unbeknownst to the numismatic world, for generations. The set contained examples of U.S. proof coins from the early 19th century, and though most were dated 1834, two of them—including the silver dollar—bore the date 1804.

The researchers discovered that special U.S. proof sets were made in the early 1830s as gifts for Asian rulers. The sets were to be presented—although just two of them were—when a U.S. trade envoy visited those rulers' far-off lands in hopes of forging economic ties. From their dates, it is clear that the coins were meant to be current-year issues. But silver dollars and eagles ($10 gold pieces), though still considered part of the nation's coinage lineup, hadn't been issued since 1804. The U.S. Mint's solution, the researchers suggested, was to strike new examples of those coins but date them 1804.

That explained why the Siam set, made in the 1830s, contained a silver dollar dated 1804. But what about those 19,570 dollars produced by the Mint in 1804? Again, the researchers had a logical answer: Since it was the Mint's practice at that time to use coinage dies until they wore out, even after the end of a calendar year, the coins almost certainly were struck from dies left over from 1803. So the 1804 dollars made for the special sets three decades later were the only ones actually struck with that date.

The King of Siam specimen is one of eight "original" 1804 dollars identified by numismatic scholars. There also are seven restrikes made by the Mint in the late 1850s to satisfy collector demand. All would undoubtedly sell for a million dollars or more if offered for sale today.

In addition to all the mystique surrounding these remarkable rarities, the Siam set has a literary connection. After being given to Siam's King Rama III in 1836, the set was handed down to the monarch's son, Rama IV, the subject of the book and play *Anna and the King of Siam* and the Rodgers and Hammerstein musical *The King and I*. And he, in turn, is believed to have given it to the British governess Anna Leonowens—the "Anna" in the book and Broadway shows. After her death in 1915, the set is said to have remained a family heirloom until the late 1950s, when it was sold to a London coin dealer. Since then, the set's value has skyrocketed: In a private transaction in November 2005, California coin dealer Steven L. Contursi reportedly purchased it for $8.5 million.

With so many facets and such an incredible history, the 1804 silver dollar is a consummate winner. And unlike the 1933 Saint-Gaudens double eagle, it doesn't have a possible overhang to make potential buyers uneasy. The number of pieces available is well established, and though it's extremely small, it's large enough to offer hope to prosperous collectors that one day they may own one.

There may be lingering questions about this coin's murky origins, but there's absolutely no mystery as to why it is has become an enduring symbol of numismatic nobility.

Simply stated, the 1804 dollar possesses the very essence of a great collector coin.

LOSER

4

The 1792 half disme

The coin we call the "nickel" is such a familiar part of our lives that we hardly ever give it a second look—or a second thought. We don't stop to question why it's so much larger than the dime, a coin with twice the value. Or why it's called a "nickel" when its composition is actually 75 percent copper and only 25 percent nickel. It would come as a great surprise to most Americans to learn that for three-quarters of a century, the U.S. Mint didn't even produce such a coin, and people made do instead with a small silver five-cent piece called the "half dime."

As its name suggests, the half dime was precisely half the weight of the dime and the same metallic composition, a more logical arrangement (although a less practical one) than what we have today. The nickel five-cent piece proved more convenient and therefore more popular when it was introduced in 1866, and the half dime was abolished seven years later. But when it first appeared, the small silver coin saw widespread use in commerce and suited our forefathers' taste for coinage with high intrinsic value.

The very first half dime is looked upon by many as the first U.S. coin of any kind. It was struck in the cellar of a Philadelphia home in July 1792—months before the opening of the nation's first mint in that city. Notwithstanding the location, the 1,500 pieces made at that time had congressional authorization. What's more, they were minted from silverplate provided by President George Washington. These coins bear the inscription **HALF DISME,** *disme* being French for "tenth" (as in tenth of a dollar).

The Mint later anglicized this to *dime*. The 1792 half disme is rare, historic, and desirable.

This coin was long considered a winner, but the price has advanced to the point at which I have no choice but to proclaim it a loser. High-grade circulated examples advanced in value considerably in the eight years since the first edition of this book—from $35,000 to $250,000. Less than a decade ago, a Gem example was priced at $250,000; today a Gem would cost you $1.5 million.

WINNER
5

The 1856 Flying Eagle cent in Proof-63, 64, or 65

The Lincoln cent has been around so long that most of us can't imagine life without it; introduced in 1909, it has outlasted the vast majority of the U.S. population alive at that time. The cent hasn't always carried Abraham Lincoln's portrait, though. In fact, it hasn't always been the size it is today. For more than 60 years, from the start of U.S. coinage to the eve of the Civil War, the cent was a large, bulky coin—almost the size of today's half dollar—and was made not of bronze, brass, or copper-plated zinc, like most Lincoln cents, but rather of pure copper.

By the 1850s, the large copper cent had worn out its welcome, along with the pockets of many Americans, because it was so heavy and inconvenient to carry around. The U.S. Mint conducted tests to find a suitable substitute and settled at length on a much smaller coin made from an alloy of 88 percent copper and 12 percent nickel. The coin was the same diameter as the current Lincoln cent but thicker and nearly twice as heavy. It carried a portrait showing an eagle in flight and came to be known as the Flying Eagle cent.

The Flying Eagle cent wasn't struck for commerce until 1857. However, the Mint produced small quantities of the coin in 1856 for presentation to members of Congress, Treasury officials, and other dignitaries, partly to show them what it had in mind and partly to win their support. Researchers estimate that more than 600 were distributed in this fashion and that hundreds of restrikes were made a few years later, using the same dies, for sale to collectors of the day—a combined total of possibly 1,500, all of them proofs. The 1856 Flying Eagle cent has always been popular with collectors and doubtless always will be. Besides being rare, it's also the nation's first small-size cent. Prices are far from cheap—$20,000 in Proof-63, $25,000 in Proof-64, and $30,000 in Proof-65—but this coin will always be worth a pretty penny.

An uncirculated roll of 1950-D Jefferson nickels

At first glance, the 1950-D Jefferson nickel appears to be a real bargain. Its mintage of just over 2.6 million is the lowest in the entire Jefferson series, a series that dates back to 1938. And as of late 2006, a roll of 40 uncirculated 1950-D nickels was retailing for less than $500—a fraction of what it would have brought in the early 1960s, when the market value peaked at $1,200 per roll.

The fact is, however, that even at such a seemingly depressed price level, a roll of '50-D nickels is no bargain. True, the mintage is low, at least by the standards of this series, but collectors were aware of this at the time the coin was issued, so they hoarded rolls and even bags of this nickel. As a consequence, a very high percentage of the 2.6 million examples ended up being preserved in mint condition. It may very well be, in fact, that this coin is scarcer in circulation condition than it is brand new.

In all likelihood, the 1950-D nickel is more common in mint condition than numerous other Jeffersons from around the same period whose mintages are considerably higher, since those coins weren't set aside to nearly the same extent when they were new. There is serious doubt whether it even merits its current market value of roughly $7 per coin. And purchasing it in roll quantities makes little sense, as that just multiplies the potential overpayment 40 times. Buying rolls of uncirculated late-date coins was all the rage in the early 1960s, but that approach has been discredited by their generally dismal performance during the intervening years.

The 1926-S Buffalo nickel graded Mint State-64

Everybody loves the Buffalo nickel. This ruggedly handsome coin is pure Americana—the embodiment of America's frontier past and the rough-and-tumble, romanticized era that saw this nation fulfill its "manifest destiny." Collectors are no exceptions: Few, if any, U.S. coins enjoy such a solid base of dedicated enthusiasts in the hobby.

Oddly, the most expensive coins in this series are offbeat varieties, rather than standard date-and-mint issues. The 1916 nickel with a doubled-die obverse and the 1918-D overdate, with the 8 engraved over a 7, both command five-figure prices in mint condition. The 1937-D "three-legged" nickel, with a missing foreleg on the bison, isn't far behind on the price charts. The standard issues do have their share of scarce and desirable collectibles, however. The three most challenging coins in this group are low-mintage nickels struck in the 1920s in San Francisco: the 1921-S, 1924-S, and 1926-S. And of these three, the 1926-S is head and shoulders (plus tail and haunches) above the rest.

To start with, the 1926-S is the lowest-mintage coin in the Buffalo nickel series (not counting oddball varieties). At 970,000, it's the only coin in the series with a mintage below 1 million. And, to compound its rarity, it's notorious for being weakly struck. Sharply struck examples are few and far between, and when they do turn up, they bring impressive premiums. You'd be hard-pressed to find an example of this date in grades of Mint State-65 and above, and you'd have to pay dearly to obtain one. Even in Mint State-64, the price is steep: upwards of $10,000. That would be money well spent, though, for when you combine the great popularity of Buffalo nickels in general with the genuine rarity of the 1926-S and then add attractive mint condition, you have a surefire formula for future appreciation.

The 1938-D Buffalo nickel graded Mint State-67

Appearances can be deceiving. The 1938-D Buffalo nickel is a classic case in point. At first glance, this coin seems to be the numismatic equivalent of the guy who has everything: Its mintage is relatively low, at just over 7 million; it's almost always sharply struck and aesthetically appealing—even dazzling—and it's part of a coinage series that perennially ranks as one of the most popular, in fact, one of the most beloved, in all of American history. Despite all these positive attributes, though, this is one of the lowest-priced coins in the Buffalo nickel series. Its value is so modest, in fact, that you have to go all the way up the scale to Mint State-67—what some describe as a "super-grade" coin—before its price tag tops $300.

It must perplex the uninitiated to look at a price list and see the 1938-D Buffalo running neck and neck with the 1936, a nickel whose mintage of 119 million is 14 times higher. The puzzlement can only be compounded by the fact that a number of Buffaloes with comparably low mintages—the 1919-D, 1919-S, 1920-D, and 1925-S, for example—bring much higher premiums right across the board than the '38-D, particularly in pristine mint condition.

In a sense, what we have here is too much of a good thing. Unlike the earlier branch-mint nickels just mentioned, the 1938-D was set aside by collectors in very substantial quantities immediately after its release. In large part, that's because this was the final coin in the Buffalo series; the Jefferson nickel took its place later the same year, and widespread publicity about the impending change had alerted the nation's hobbyists, and noncollectors, too, and prompted many to save both kinds by the roll and even the bag. Also, while its sharpness makes the 1938-D more attractive than many earlier branch-mint Buffaloes, it also makes the coin readily available in even the highest grades, which, under the law of supply and demand, depresses its value. Some of the earlier coins are impossible to find with razor-sharp strikes; by contrast, the '38-D is almost impossible to find *without* such a strike. Given all this, I'd steer clear of the '38-D. That MS-67 piece really isn't a bargain at $300. There are just too many fish in this particular sea—or rather, too many bison on this plain. The combined NGC and PCGS population figures for this coin in MS-67 are 2,633 coins as of October 2006.

WINNER
7

The 1955 doubled-die Lincoln cent graded Mint State-63

Everybody makes mistakes, and the U.S. Mint is no exception. Despite its determined efforts at quality control, the Mint produces coins with obvious imperfections now and then, and though it catches many of these before they get away, others find their way into general circulation and end up as intriguing conversation pieces. They also end up as coveted collectibles, avidly pursued by a large and growing body of "error coin" enthusiasts nationwide.

One of the biggest "boo-boos" ever to escape from Uncle Sam's clutches was a 1955 Lincoln cent with dramatically doubled images on the date and the inscriptions on the obverse. This error came about because of misalignment in a process known as "hubbing" of the dies. A coin is created by striking a *planchet*, or blank piece of metal, with two dies—one bearing the design for the obverse, the other having the elements for the reverse. On each die, the design appears in mirror image. A die, in turn, is made by striking a piece of tempered steel with a hub, a harder piece of steel on which the design is positive, or just the way it will look on the finished coin. To make the impression stronger, technicians give each master die multiple blows with the hub. On rare occasions, the hub and die become misaligned between blows, and when that occurs, the die emerges with doubling of the images. That's what happened in 1955.

Inspectors discovered this problem, but not before small but significant quantities of "doubled-die" cents—perhaps 30,000—had been mixed with normal coins. Rather than destroy the whole batch, they decided to let the misstrikes go. This was a bonanza for collectors, for the coins soon became sought-after prizes. Most entered circulation, however briefly, and mint state examples are extremely scarce. Given this small supply and the great demand for these coins, they're well worth the going price of $3,500 in Mint State-63. They have nowhere to go but up.

LOSER
7 ⬇ The 1995 doubled-die Lincoln cent graded
Mint State-67

Collectors across the country got out their magnifying glasses in the spring of 1995, when they learned of an exciting new discovery: Brand-new Lincoln cents dated 1995 were turning up with doubling on the obverse, or "heads," side. It wasn't as sharp and obvious as some of the earlier "doubled-die" errors had been, but it was clear enough, especially when viewed under even low-power magnification. The doubling was most apparent on the letters of the word LIBERTY.

Reports about these coins soon began appearing not only in hobby newspapers and magazines but also in general-interest periodicals. Most impressively, *USA Today* ran a story and a photograph on its front page. The treasure hunt was on—and many of the treasure hunters ended up hitting pay dirt as they looked through bags and rolls of uncirculated cents. The 1995 doubled-die cent wasn't as dramatic as its 1955 and 1972 counterparts, but it seemed to have been struck in much more meaningful numbers and distributed much more widely.

This was a good-news, bad-news situation. The coin's availability made it easier for hobbyists to find one in circulation and add it to their collections for an outlay of just one cent. On the other hand, it exerted increasingly downward pressure on the value of the coin as the law of supply and demand took effect. Typical examples of the coin, grading perhaps Mint State-63, had been selling for about $200 apiece in the beginning, but ended up being worth less than $25. As this is written, MS-67 pieces still carry a price tag of about $100—but given the extent of the supply, I would not buy one at that level. The price almost surely is headed even lower.

WINNER
8

The 1913-S Variety 2 Buffalo nickel graded Mint State-64

The winning of America's Old West was a saga that combined triumph and tragedy. One of its greatest tragedies was the slaughter of the vast herds of American bison—popularly known as buffalo—that had roamed the range just a few decades earlier. Those herds were decimated by white settlers, who killed the animals for food, clothing, and sometimes just for sport. In 1850, it was estimated that 20 million head of buffalo populated the Western plains; by 1894, the number was barely 1,000. This loss was keenly felt by many Americans, and the buffalo came to symbolize the passing of an era in the West. This admiration, in turn, helped make the Buffalo nickel an immensely popular coin when the U.S. Mint introduced it in 1913.

The very first examples of this chiseled-looking coin were different from those that followed in a subtle yet significant way: The bison was depicted standing atop raised ground—what collectors refer to as a "mound." This reinforced the naturalistic appearance of the coin. Unfortunately, though, designer James Earle Fraser had chosen this location for the crucial inscription FIVE CENTS, and because this part of the coin was relatively high and exposed, that statement of value soon began wearing off in circulation. To correct this problem, the Mint did away with the mound, showing the bison instead on a straight line or "plain," with the words FIVE CENTS recessed below it.

Buffalo nickels were made in both varieties that year at all three mints then in operation: Philadelphia, Denver, and San Francisco. The scarcest of these was the "plain" variety from San Francisco, with a mintage of barely 1.2 million. The S-mint "mound" variety also is scarce, with a mintage of only about 2.1 million. But this was saved in far greater numbers in mint condition because it was the first to appear; when the second version came out, many saw no reason to set it aside. The 1913-S Variety 2 nickel is far from cheap; in Mint State-64, it will cost you roughly $1,800. It's worth the money, though, because it is extremely elusive in higher grades.

LOSER
8

The 1913 Variety 1 Buffalo nickel graded Mint State-66

The "mound"-type Buffalo nickel has much to recommend it. To begin with, it's a one-year type coin; only the very first coins in this series—those produced in the early months of 1913—show the bison (or buffalo) standing atop raised ground. By April of that year, Mint officials realized that the words FIVE CENTS—engraved on the mound—were wearing off quickly in circulation, and they moved to correct this by leveling the surface underneath the buffalo and recessing, and protecting, the statement of value. Beyond that, the so-called Variety 1 nickels possess a rough-hewn surface that is missing on subsequent pieces, and many collectors consider them aesthetically more appealing. Mint technicians needlessly smoothed out the design's details at the same time they were making the needed modification of the mound.

Given all this, one might assume that Variety 1 Buffaloes would command hefty premiums. This assumption would seem even safer upon examination of the coins' mintage figures, for these are only marginally higher than those of the "plain"-type nickels of 1913. At the Philadelphia Mint, for example, production levels were virtually the same for the two varieties: not quite 31 million nickels with the mound, and not quite 30 million with the straight line under the buffalo.

In point of fact, however, Variety 1 nickels are far more available in pristine mint condition than those of Variety 2. That's because they came out first, so they were the ones most people set aside as mementos. By the time the modified version appeared, the Buffalo nickel had been around for months and people were getting used to it, so the novelty—like the inscription—was wearing off. The modification is meaningful to collectors, but it held no special significance to many in the noncollecting public. Variety 1 Buffaloes are certainly desirable, especially in high levels of preservation, but you must be careful not to overpay for them. The going price of $350 for the Philadelphia nickel in Mint State-66 strikes me as too high for a coin that is really not that scarce. As of October 2006, the combined population number for this coin in MS-66 graded by NGC and PCGS was 2,427 pieces.

WINNER
9 ⬆

Proof-66 nickel three-cent pieces

The U.S. coinage lineup is highly compact today. Even with the addition of a new dollar coin in the year 2000, the nation entered the new millennium with just six circulating coin denominations—and one of those, the half dollar, sees little or no use in circulation. By contrast, Americans had more than a dozen coin varieties at their disposal during much of the 19th century, including different coins of the same denomination. For a brief period after the Civil War, the U.S. Mint was making two kinds of five-cent pieces (one in nickel, the other in silver), two different three-cent pieces (also in nickel and silver), and two different dollar coins (one in gold and one in silver).

Today, it seems odd to think of having a three-cent piece at all, much less two kinds. This curious denomination first came into being in 1851, when the Mint began producing the silver version—a small, wafer-thin coin intended to simplify the purchase of postage stamps, whose basic rate was then being lowered from five cents to three. The silver three-cent piece proved impractical, though, because of its tiny size, and in 1865, under pressure from nickel-mining interests, Congress approved a new kind made of 75 percent copper and 25 percent nickel—the same alloy used in the Jefferson nickel today.

The nickel three-cent piece never was widely used in circulation, but it did serve a purpose by helping the federal government retire the unpopular three-cent fractional notes issued as emergency money during the Civil War. The coin was discontinued in 1889, after more than a decade of generally very low mintages. But, while the public may not have embraced it at the time, many current collectors find the coin desirable—especially in mint condition and proof. The Mint struck proofs, or specimen coins, each year of the series' life—nearly half of them in quantities of 1,000 or fewer. I particularly like them in Proof-66. The going price for such a coin is a mere $850, more than justified by the rarity.

LOSER
9

Mercury dimes from the 1940s graded Mint State-67 with full bands

Coin collectors have gotten very fussy in recent years. Whereas previous generations of hobbyists were satisfied, for the most part, with problem-free, lightly circulated coins, many collectors today will settle for nothing less than mint condition. Some insist on pristine mint condition and pay substantial premiums for the privilege of owning such high-grade coins. In some cases, this is justified because the coins in question are rare or extremely scarce in such condition. In other cases, however, substantial numbers exist in grades above Mint State-65, so disproportionate premiums are unwarranted.

One of the byproducts of quality consciousness has been a heavy emphasis on whether certain coins are sharply struck in designated areas. These are areas that normally exhibit weakness, so if they are fully struck, the coins are deemed to be superior examples and often command impressive premiums. For instance, Miss Liberty's head tends to be weakly struck on Standing Liberty quarters, so "full-head" examples are highly prized and often very high-priced.

Over the years, collectors have observed that Winged Liberty (or "Mercury") dimes have weakness, as a rule, in portions of the fasces on the reverse. This device—a symbol of authority in Roman times—consists of a bundle of rods bound around an ax, and by rights there should be separation in the bands that bind the bundle. But only the sharpest specimens possess this separation, so "full-bands" Mercury dimes are looked upon as scarce and worth a premium. Beware of paying big premiums, though, for full-bands dimes from the 1940s. Unlike earlier issues, many of these were sharply struck, so the premium, if any, should be nominal. The current price of $175 for PCGS MS-67 examples with full bands is excessive. The 1944-D in MS-67 with full bands, just one example from this period, has a combined total population from NGC and PCGS of 1,900 pieces, so clearly these coins, even in MS-67, are far from rare.

The 1909-S Lincoln cent graded Extremely Fine or better

The Lincoln cent is taken for granted today by most Americans. But when it first appeared in 1909, it was really quite revolutionary: Up to that time, no U.S. coin minted for use in commerce ever had portrayed a real-life person from the nation's past. The coin was conceived as a tribute to Abraham Lincoln on the 100th anniversary of his birth, and while its simple portrait may seem commonplace today, it represented a breakthrough artistically, as well, in 1909, for up to then U.S. coinage had been heavily allegorical. This, by contrast, was handsomely realistic.

When coin collectors think of the very first Lincoln cents, they tend to focus on those bearing the letters "VDB." The coin's designer, Victor David Brenner, had placed those letters (his initials) at the base of the reverse as a kind of artistic signature. It is common practice for coin designers' initials to appear on their creations: James Longacre's "L" can be found on the bonnet ribbon on the Indian Head cent, for example, and Charles Barber's "B" is etched on Miss Liberty's shoulder on the Barber silver coins. But those are rather small and inconspicuous. Brenner's three initials seemed to jump right off the coin, prompting public protest and leading to their removal soon after production got under way.

The San Francisco Mint had struck only 484,000 Lincoln cents before the initials were removed. The 1909-S VDB cent turned out to be the lowest-mintage coin in the whole Lincoln series, not counting errors and varieties, and has been a prized collectible ever since. The West Coast mint went on to produce 1,825,000 cents without the designer's initials in 1909, and while these are far less publicized, they're still extremely scarce and desirable. You can expect to pay about $180 for a 1909-S cent graded Extremely Fine, and several times as much for one that is Mint State-63, but this is a scarce issue in a highly popular series—even without the VDB.

The 1931-S Lincoln cent graded Mint State-65

"Brother, Can You Spare a Dime?" That became the theme song of the Great Depression for millions of Americans who found themselves with no jobs, no money, and little or no hope that prosperity, or even recovery, would really be around the next corner. Hardly anyone had a dime to spare, or even a red cent, including the U.S. Mint, where production fell to its lowest ebb in the 20th century. The Mint made gold coins every year till 1933, but few of those were distributed, much less used. Other than those, the Mint issued only cents, nickels, and dimes in 1931; cents and quarters in 1932; and cents and half dollars in 1933. New coins were superfluous at a time when so many people couldn't afford to spend them.

Lincoln cents were minted every year, but at very low levels. Production hit rock-bottom at the San Francisco Mint in 1931, when just 866,000 cents were struck all year long. That's the second-lowest mintage of any Lincoln cent, not counting errors and varieties, topped (or rather, bottomed) only by the 1909-S VDB, whose output totaled just 484,000. But whereas the 1909-S VDB circulated widely, and thus is extremely scarce in mint condition, the 1931-S saw little or no use in commerce. The lack of demand for circulating coinage was one obvious reason. Beyond that, however, the coin's low mintage became common knowledge among collectors, and much of the supply was set aside before it even entered circulation. One old-time dealer reported being offered a chance to buy roughly half the total mintage—some 500,000 pieces—at one time from a Western bank.

The 1931-S cent carries a price tag of nearly $650 in Mint State-65 Red—meaning the coin still displays the same vibrant red color it was manufactured with—and the figure gets rather fancy in grades above that. Thousands and thousands exist in mint condition, however, so you should be wary of paying a big premium for this coin. It's a classic case in which despite a low mintage, the available supply is still quite ample.

WINNER
11 ⬆

Type 3 Liberty double eagles graded Proof-65

David Hall, the highly astute founder of the Professional Coin Grading Service, commented once that "only real men collect proof gold." His point was that proof U.S. gold coins are rare and expensive right across the board, so only people with lots of buying power—and the willingness to risk large sums of money—can afford to dabble, much less take a full-scale plunge, in this high-stakes corner of the marketplace. Every proof gold coin is, quite literally, a trophy to be cherished and savored.

Proof gold coins are dazzling in any denomination—but because of their size and heft, proof double eagles (or $20 gold pieces) represent the ultimate in mint-making magnificence. These large, heavy coins contain very nearly an ounce of gold and, as proofs, they are superior—sometimes superb—specimens both technically and aesthetically.

Saint-Gaudens double dagles get the most attention, but I have always been partial to the Liberty gold $20s that preceded "Saints" in the U.S. coinage lineup. These elegant-looking coins are rooted in the mid-19th century, and their issuance spanned a period of more than half a century, during which the nation fought and survived a bloody civil war, won the American West, and literally expanded from sea to shining sea. Collectors divide Liberty $20s into three types. From 1849 to 1866, the coins lacked the motto IN GOD WE TRUST; the motto then appeared until the end of the series in 1907, and from 1877 till the end, the statement of value was shown as TWENTY DOLLARS, rather than TWENTY D. This last group, known as Type 3, is the one I especially recommend. A Proof-65 example will cost you about $100,000—but with mintages ranging from a low of 20 to a high of just 158, these coins are not only dazzling but also downright rare. Real men—and women—will always desire them.

An uncirculated roll of 1960 small-date Lincoln cents

Lincoln cents have always been enormously popular with collectors. Their low face value makes them extremely affordable for even the youngest collectors—armed with just a modest weekly allowance— to collect them from circulation. Plus, scarcer-date issues and interesting varieties can—and do—turn up in pocket change. Back in 1960, the U.S. Mint produced a Lincoln cent that combined these two elements: a scarce coin that was also an interesting variety. It touched off a treasure hunt that brought many thousands of new collectors into the hobby. That coin was the 1960 small-date cent.

Normally, the Mint changes just one number—the last one—on the master dies for its coins at the start of each calendar year. But once every 10 years, at the start of a new decade, it has to change the second-to-last number, as well. That's what happened in 1960. Soon after the start of production, Mint technicians noticed that the numbers on the new cents were becoming clogged. To correct the problem, they made the numbers larger. In doing so, they unwittingly created a scarce and popular variety. As collectors soon discovered, the early strikes—those with a "small" date—were readily distinguishable from the later ones, and a great deal harder to find.

Small-date cents were made at both mints then in operation, Philadelphia and Denver, but those from Philadelphia were particularly elusive. Researchers estimate that no more than a few million examples were produced there, and at one time, these were selling for $400 or more per roll of 50 uncirculated pieces. As of this writing, the price is about $175 per roll, and I see little likelihood that it will rise significantly in the foreseeable future. This is an interesting variety, and many collectors include it in their Lincoln cent collections, but while it's scarce, it's available. And virtually every example was saved in mint condition without ever reaching circulation, so there's little or no premium on high quality.

A 1936 Walking Liberty half dollar graded Proof-65

Whenever collectors and connoisseurs of coinage art draw up lists of America's loveliest coins, the Walking Liberty half dollar never fails to rank among their top selections. This stunningly beautiful coin is truly a numismatic masterpiece, and many observers place it at or near the top of their lists, along with the Saint-Gaudens double eagle. The U.S. Mint apparently agrees, for in 1986 it chose the obverse portrait from the Walking Liberty coin, with its full-length view of Miss Liberty, for the obverse of the American Eagle silver bullion coin. The Saint-Gaudens design was chosen for the gold American Eagle, so this was a powerful statement that in the government's view, the "Walker" stands at the head of the class among U.S. silver coins, just as the exquisite "Saint" does among the gold.

The magnificence of the design is shown to greatest advantage on proof specimens, on which multiple striking captures each delicate detail and subtle nuance, and where there is maximum contrast between the frosty devices (or raised design areas) and the highly polished fields (or background portions). Proof Walking Liberty halves are among the most breathtaking coins Uncle Sam ever made.

Although the series lasted for more than three decades, from 1916 through 1947, proofs were struck for public sale in only seven years—from 1936 through 1942. And while the number of proofs was modest throughout that span, it was easily the lowest in 1936, when the Mint produced just 3,901. You'll pay a pretty penny for the privilege of owning one: In Proof-65, this coin carries a price tag of about $6,000. But you'll have a coin possessing exceptional beauty, extremely high quality, and very low mintage—a rare combination indeed.

Common-date Walking Liberty half dollars graded Mint State-66 or 67

Rarity and quality are attributes that enhance the value of a coin as a collectible. They might be described as twin towers. When a coin possesses both of these characteristics, its value can be very great indeed. When it possesses neither, its value is likely to be relatively small. But what about a coin that has one of these two attributes, but lacks the other? Determining the value of such a mixed-bag coin can require specialized knowledge, broad experience, and, most important of all, common sense.

Complicating matters is a factor called "condition rarity." Certain coins are common in circulated condition, or even lower levels of mint condition, but scarce or even rare in very high levels of preservation. This is true, for instance, of some coins in the Morgan dollar series. Take the 1886-O silver dollar, for example. This coin has a mintage of more than 10 million and is readily available in circulated condition. Its value soars, however, in mint condition, and especially in grades of Mint State-63 and above.

This brings us to another popular U.S. silver coin—the Walking Liberty half dollar. The lowest-mintage coins in this series—the three half dollars of 1921, the 1916, the 1916-S with the mint mark on the obverse, and the 1938-D—command a meaningful premium, a premium based on rarity, even in lower grades. Some of the coins with somewhat higher mintages command significant premiums in the higher grades—because of condition rarity. Relatively few exist in such high grades. In both of these examples, the premiums are justified. All too often, though, dealers put high price tags on common-date Walking halves based entirely on their quality, even though rarity—and condition rarity—is not a factor. Many of these coins, especially those from the later years in the series, are really quite abundant even in grades as high as Mint State-66 ($200) or 67 ($600). Don't let their pretty faces fool you—and don't pay their fancy prices.

WINNER

13

Franklin half dollars graded Mint State-66 or higher

The Franklin half dollar first appeared at about the same time as the baby boom generation of Americans. And under normal circumstances, it—like the baby boomers—might still be a highly visible part of the scene today. Events conspired, however, to cut short the life of this interesting coin after only 15 years of production.

Under legislation enacted in 1890, regular-issue U.S. coins (the kind meant for use in everyday circulation) can't be replaced until they have been minted for at least 25 years. But Congress has the power to override this law if it so chooses, and that's what it opted to do during the closing days of 1963. Emotions were high following the assassination of President John F. Kennedy on November 22 of that year, and sentiment was strong to honor the slain president on a U.S. coin. For various reasons, Congress selected the half dollar as the vehicle, so the Franklin half dollar, introduced in 1948, suffered a premature death a decade before the coin would have reached the statutory minimum age. Even then, existing Franklin halves normally would have lingered in circulation for many years, but in 1965, when the Mint began producing "clad" cupro-nickel coins, older silver coins quickly disappeared into hoarders' hands.

There are no major rarities in the Franklin half dollar series—at least not in terms of the quantities made; the lowest-mintage issues, the Philadelphia halves of 1953 and 1955, both were minted in numbers approaching 3 million. But specialists have found that many Franklin halves are extremely hard to find—sometimes almost impossible—in very high grades with full, sharp strikes. The design is deceptively simple, with Benjamin Franklin's portrait and the likeness of the Liberty Bell both having clean, open looks. But subtle details are missing from most of these coins, even in mint condition; few, for example, display full lines on the bell. Franklin half dollars are common in grades of Mint State-63 and below; in higher grades, however, they command substantial premiums, generally much more than $100, and based on their scarcity, they're well worth it.

Prices can reach into the thousands of dollars depending on the specific coin.

LOSER
13

Susan B. Anthony dollars graded Proof-69 or 70

The Susan B. Anthony dollar is a quintessential "loser"—perhaps the biggest loser in the annals of U.S. coinage. This singularly unloved and unlamented coin was conceived as a convenience for American consumers: It gave them a small-size, high-value coin for use in such devices as vending machines, pay phones, and toll-collection baskets—or so the reasoning went. At the same time, it had the potential to make a small fortune for Uncle Sam. That's because each "Susie" cost just pennies to produce but went on the books as a dollar when it entered circulation, giving the federal government a profit of roughly 97 cents per coin in what is known as "seigniorage."

In theory, it couldn't miss. But in practice, this coin, with its curiously ugly portrait of suffragette Anthony, was a failure from the outset. People found it aesthetically unattractive, saw no reason to switch to this newfangled coin from good old dollar bills, and, most telling of all, had a hard time distinguishing it from the only slightly smaller Washington quarter. Besides being close in size to the 25-cent piece, the Anthony dollar had the same composition and thus the same physical appearance. Anybody who spent one in place of a quarter, thereby incurring a 75-cent loss, became an unremitting enemy of the coin.

Unpopularity notwithstanding, certain Anthony dollars do command premiums on some dealers' price sheets. Specimens graded Proof-69 or 70 by grading services, for example, appear on home shopping programs with price tags above $100. Ostensibly, this is because Susies are hard to come by in very high grades, but, in fact, they are not rare in Proof-69 or 70. Even the business-strike Anthony dollars tend to be decently struck, and many—indeed, most—proofs have survived in their original state of preservation because they were issued in highly protective packaging. All in all, they're just losers.

WINNER
14 ⬆

Mint State 1809–1837 Capped Bust dimes

Age is relative. To most present-day Americans, movies, songs, and, yes, U.S. coins from before World War II seem old and dated. They are, after all, six decades or more in the past, and 60 years in human terms represents close to a full lifetime. Those same pre-war coins look a lot more modern, though when viewed alongside such truly old coins as Capped Bust U.S. dimes from the early 1800s. Those coins pre-date not only World War II but also the Civil War and, for that matter, the Mexican-American War.

The dime was among the basic denominations authorized by Congress in the Mint Act of 1792, but it was among the last of those coins to enter production, not being issued until 1796. The earliest dimes were slightly larger and heavier than their modern counterparts and were made from an alloy containing slightly less than 90 percent silver; since 1965, dimes have been devoid of precious metal. The very first dimes had what is known as a "Draped Bust" design, showing a bust of Miss Liberty with drapery over her shoulder. In 1809, this portrait was modified and a turban-type cap was placed on Liberty's head, creating what is known as the Capped Bust dime. This design continued until 1837, when the coin's dimensions were slenderized, giving it the diameter still in use today.

Capped Bust dimes had extremely low mintages, judged by current standards. In only four years did their output exceed 1 million, and then not by much. On the other hand, there were nine years in which the total came to less than 500,000. Furthermore, few were saved, since coin collectors were similarly sparse in those early years. You can expect to spend close to $600 for the "small size" (1828–37) and $1,000 for the "large size" (1809–28), even for specimens graded just Mint State-60, and several times as much for one that grades MS-63. But these coins are legitimately scarce and well worth the premiums they bring.

A complete set of U.S. Olympic coins from any given year

More than 110 years have passed since the modern Olympic Games took place for the very first time in 1896 in Athens, Greece. During that time, the Games have evolved into a global extravaganza—a spectacle that serves as a showcase and a springboard for the greatest amateur athletes in the world and, at the same time, cloaks their athletic achievements in a mantle of national pride. Today, there are Olympics every two years, with Summer Games and Winter Games both on four-year timetables in alternating even-numbered years.

Initially, the Games were relatively modest in scope. As time went by, however, they became increasingly elaborate and expensive, placing a heavy burden on host countries and cities and causing them to seek new means by which to raise the needed revenues. Television and radio rights have proved to be a lucrative source of such funds, as has the sale of marketing rights to large corporations that flaunt the Olympic symbol and proclaim themselves to be "proud sponsors" of the Games. And so, in recent decades, has the sale of collector coins that issuers declare to be official Olympic issues.

The United States hosted a number of Olympics, both Summer and Winter, in the first 84 years of the modern Games. But the first U.S. Olympic coins didn't appear until 1984, when three special coins authorized by Congress marked and helped finance the Los Angeles Summer Games. Since then, the U.S. Mint has issued such coins routinely for every new Summer Olympiad—even when the Games took place on foreign soil. Typically, their issue price includes a hefty surcharge earmarked for Olympic-related programs. You could pay hundreds—or even thousands—of dollars to get complete sets of these coins. But given their high mintages and high issue prices, your only reward is likely to be the inner glow of being a proud Olympic sponsor—and subsidizer.

The advent of the State Quarters program and popularity of modern coins has propelled some of these less common sets to higher price levels, which is all the more reason to stay away from overpriced losers that could decline in value as quickly as they increased.

WINNER
15

An Isabella quarter graded Mint State-65

The U.S. Mint was 100 years old before it began producing commemorative coinage as most collectors understand that term—coinage that is issued to honor a particular person, place, or event and sold at a premium to help raise funds for a worthy cause. The event that brought the first such coins into being was the World's Columbian Exposition, a world's fair held in Chicago to commemorate the 400th anniversary of Christopher Columbus's voyage of discovery to America.

The Columbian Exposition was a highly ambitious venture involving the creation of a virtual new city along the shore of Lake Michigan, complete with 160 buildings and 65,000 exhibits showcasing Americans' impressive advances in architecture, art, science, technology, and other fields of human endeavor. The project ended up costing some $30 million—more than $1 for each of the 28 million visitors it attracted. That may sound piddling today, but at that time a dollar constituted much of a day's pay for many Americans. To help defray these costs, the managers of the fair requested, and received, congressional authorization for special U.S. coins they could sell as souvenirs to raise funds.

Initially, Congress authorized just one coin: a half dollar bearing the likeness of Columbus. Some 2.5 million examples of this "Columbian half dollar" were minted in 1892 and again in 1893, and today they are considered quite common. A few months later, however, the exposition's Board of Lady Managers sought a separate coin reflecting women's role in the fair and in society as a whole. Congress responded by authorizing a 25-cent piece bearing the image of Spain's Queen Isabella, who, with her husband, Ferdinand, financed Columbus' expedition. Just 40,000 examples of this "Isabella quarter" were minted, and more than 25,000 later were melted. Today, it is a scarce and coveted coin, and while an example graded MS-65 will cost you more than $4,000, this is a highly desirable coin with excellent upside potential.

LOSER

15 ⬇ Proof-70 American Eagles sold for tens of thousands of dollars

Precious-metal coins can be valuable on two levels. At a minimum, they are worth the value of the metal they contain. Beyond that, they can bring an additional premium—potentially a large one—based upon their value as collectibles. Common-date gold and silver coins in average circulated condition are priced on the basis of how much gold or silver they contain. Scarcer gold and silver coins generally are priced according to their numismatic, or collector, value, with intrinsic worth (their value as precious metal) providing a floor.

In recent years, some government mints have issued what are known as "bullion coins." These are official coins with legal-tender value—but unlike regular coins intended for circulation, these are meant primarily to serve as stores of value for their purchasers. They are designed to be saved, rather than spent. Among the more familiar gold bullion coins are South Africa's Krugerrand, Canada's Maple Leaf, and Great Britain's Britannia. In 1986, the United States entered the bullion-coin market with a series of gold and silver coins known as American Eagles. Dealers sell these to the public at a modest premium over their value as metal—a markup that covers the costs of production, distribution, and marketing. Their price goes up or down in direct proportion to rises or falls in the value of precious metal.

In addition to the standard American Eagles, which might be likened to business-strike coins, the Mint also offers special proof examples every year. These carry issue prices well above their value as precious metal and far above face value (which is just a small fraction of bullion value). These coins are represented as collectibles because of their sharp detail, mirror surfaces, and relatively low mintages. In reality, however, they are dolled-up bullion coins, and while they may be beautiful to behold, they're unlikely to bring you a handsome return.

In May 2006, a 1993-W American Eagle graded Proof-70 Deep Cameo by PCGS reportedly sold for $36,960 at an online auction. I consider that proof bullion coin and others like it at levels close to $40,000 to be consummate losers.

One-year type coins

Years ago, most collectors put together sets of U.S. coins according to date and mint mark. They would seek to acquire one Buffalo nickel, for example, for every date in the series and every mint that issued the coin that year. Thus, they would save three Buffalo nickels dated 1936 and three dated 1937, since production took place during those two years at three mints: Philadelphia, Denver, and San Francisco. Folders and albums sold to house sets of coins provided slots for every different "date-and-mint" combination.

In recent years, many collectors have abandoned date-and-mint collecting and turned instead to assembling sets of "type coins." Rather than encompassing every date in a series from every mint, a "type set" contains just one example of any particular coin, or one example of every major type within that series. A type set, then, might include only one Buffalo nickel, probably a high-grade specimen of a common-date issue. At most, it might include two Buffalo nickels—one with the bison on a mound, the other with the revised reverse where the mound gives way to a plain, flattened surface.

Major types are often one-year issues. Frequently, problems arise when a coin is first produced and the Mint makes adjustments to fix it before the next year's run. That's what happened in 1913, when the first Buffalo nickels proved too prone to wear on the raised mound. The problem was corrected even before that year's production ended. Since demand is high for these one-year type coins and the supply is limited to just that single year, there's strong upward pressure on their value. Some are relatively common; the Type 1 Buffalo nickel isn't a scarce issue, for example. Others are quite rare; these include the 1796 Draped Bust quarter and the 1916 Standing Liberty quarter. All, however, benefit from being one-year type coins.

1202-0332
(5) Rackateer
Nickels
1883 Gold Plated "V"
Nickels

RETAIL VALUE
$249.90
OUR PRICE
$199.95
S&H $7.99

Coins offered for sale on home-shopping television programs

Cable television has brought many changes to Americans' lifestyle, giving them programming options they never had before. One of those options is the chance to see merchandise up close and personal (and from every conceivable angle), hear it described in loving detail by rapturous (some would say *raptor-ous*) shills, and buy one or more of everything in sight simply by calling the 800 number on the screen. I'm speaking, of course, about the various home-shopping programs—and full-fledged shopping networks—that have sprung up like weeds in recent years.

Many find these programs entertaining. Some insist they've picked up great bargains by watching these shows. Perhaps they have, but based on what I've seen, those bargains haven't included collectible coins. The segments I have viewed, and the merchandise I have been shown by consumers who acquired it through these shows, leave little doubt in my mind that this is among the very worst ways to purchase coins.

By their very nature, these programs don't lend themselves to selling collector coins that are truly rare. They depend upon high-volume sales, so they have to deal in products that exist in substantial quantities. Thus, right off the bat, the coins they offer for sale are less-than-prime collectibles. Beyond that, this format is expensive for the sellers; they have to turn a profit not only for themselves but also for the people providing them with airtime—and television airtime isn't cheap. You, the consumer, end up subsidizing both these profit margins by paying excessive prices for the merchandise. These coins are often packaged very cleverly–put together in sets that stress their romantic background and their role in our nation's history. Look beyond the sizzle, though, and you will soon discover that the steak is low-grade and high-priced.

WINNER

17 ⬆

Better-date silver dollars

The year 2000 was a milestone for mankind. Few flips of the calendar involve a change in all four digits in the date. Life changed in many ways, both obvious and subtle, as the new millennium began, and one of those changes was the appearance of a new dollar coin in Americans' pocket change. It was smaller than traditional silver dollars from the nation's frontier days; instead, it was the size of the Susan B. Anthony dollar—though with crucial modifications (such as a special "golden" color) to avoid the major problems that dogged that ill-fated coin. But these new coins also appeared to be ill-fated and instead of focusing on them, collectors instead focused new attention on the full-size cartwheels of the past.

Even without a burst of new publicity, silver dollars are hardly shrinking violets. Over the last quarter-century, they have been perennial pacesetters in the coin market, with the Morgan dollar reigning as king of the hill. There are good reasons for this. These are large, bulky coins with high precious-metal content—more than three-quarters of an ounce of silver—they're old, often dating back more than a hundred years, and many are extremely well preserved, since millions never left bank and government vaults. These qualities give silver dollars exceptional appeal not only to collectors but also to investors purchasing coins for their portfolios.

Many Morgan dollars and other traditional cartwheels have bright, dazzling luster and razor-sharp detail. You need to be careful, however, not to fall in love with just a pretty face. Certain common-date dollars—the 1880-S and 1881-S, for example—exist in large quantities in pristine mint condition and really are overvalued even when purchased for a fair market price. You should concentrate instead on coins with lower mintages, even though their condition might be a bit less spectacular. They needn't be rare—only scarce. The 1886-S Morgan dollar and 1928 Peace dollar are two good examples. These coins will always be in demand, yet they're difficult to promote by offering them for sale in ads with wide circulation or on television shopping programs with high viewership because these marketers need coins available in high numbers. These are safer and sounder values.

LOSER

17

Mint State-67 commemorative coins priced far above the Mint State-66 level

Unlike regular-issue coins (the kind minted for use in everyday commerce), most commemorative coins are not produced primarily to be spent. Rather, they are meant as souvenirs, fund-raisers, mementos, and forms of national tribute. They are special coins struck for special occasions, and frequently this status is underscored by the use of fancy packaging to house them when they are issued. Uncle Sam nets a profit from selling these coins, as do organizations designated by Congress to benefit from the proceeds. The U.S. Olympic Committee, for example, has been on the receiving end several times.

The packaging and marketing were less sophisticated during the so-called "traditional" era of U.S. commemorative coinage, which extended from 1892 to 1954. Still, many of the commemoratives issued during that period did reach initial purchasers in holders that, at least, provided basic protection from wear and mishandling. Thus, when these coins were set aside in drawers or boxes or whatever, they stood a good chance of surviving in a high state of preservation, unlike regular coins, which typically lack such protection.

It stands to reason that a coin graded Mint State-67 will command a higher premium than a similar coin graded Mint State-66. It's also understandable that, in some instances, that premium may be quite substantial. Coins in certain series—and certain dates within a given series—become extremely scarce when you reach that rarified level of preservation. But different ground rules apply with commemorative coins. With them, the survival rate is considerably higher in upper mint-state levels. Therefore, the extra premium shouldn't be as great. There are exceptions, to be sure, but as a general rule, you should be wary when the price gap between these two grade levels is dramatic.

The 1915 Panama-Pacific $50 gold piece, either octagonal or round

The Panama Canal is truly a "Wonder of the Modern World"—a manmade work every bit as stupendous in its way as the pyramids of Egypt and the rest of the seven wonders of ancient times. The notion of constructing a canal across the narrow isthmus of Panama had been conceived as early as the 16th century, when Spanish conquistadors first arrived in the region. Even then, its strategic value as a navigation shortcut was apparent. France made the first attempt to build such a canal in 1880, but was forced to abandon the effort 10 years later. Congress authorized a U.S. venture in 1902 and work got under way the following year. After overcoming formidable engineering and medical obstacles, American canal-builders finished the massive project a decade later, and the waterway opened to traffic in 1914.

Americans were justifiably proud of this achievement, and to celebrate the feat, a national party was scheduled in San Francisco in 1915. Actually, the party was global in nature: It was billed as the Panama-Pacific International Exposition and was meant as a kind of grand-scale house warming—or canal warming—officially marking the opening of this wonderful new resource that would, after all, improve the lot of mankind as a whole. To mark the festive occasion and help finance its costs, Congress also authorized five special coins to be sold to the show's visitors (and others who might want them) at a premium.

The "Pan-Pac" coins included a silver half dollar, a gold dollar, a quarter eagle (or $2.50 gold piece), and two $50 gold pieces—the first U.S. coins ever issued in that denomination. The $50 coins were identical in design, both depicting the Greek goddess Minerva on the obverse and her symbol, the owl, on the reverse; one was round, however, while the other was octagonal. These coins have been acclaimed for their beauty. Even more attractive to investment-minded buyers are their mintages: After unsold specimens were melted, the net remaining figures were 685 octagonal pieces and 483 round. These coins are expensive, typically bringing strong five-figure prices. But they're rare, beautiful, desirable, and likely to continue rising in value as time goes by.

Generic Morgan dollars graded Mint State-65, 66, or 67

Morgan silver dollars hold great appeal for investors. They're also special favorites of dealers who cater to investors. There are several good reasons for this appeal: Morgan dollars are large silver coins that exude a combination of heft and intrinsic value. They are the numismatic equivalent of antiques, dating back to the 19th century in most cases, but many millions are preserved in mint condition. They represent a link to America's Old West. And, in a number of instances, they are legitimately scarce and valuable as collectibles.

But not all Morgan dollars are truly scarce, even in pristine mint condition. Some of them, on the contrary, are readily available in high Mint State grades—available by the thousands even in such a lofty grade as Mint State-66. That's because vast quantities of these cartwheels never saw use in commerce; after being minted, they sat for generations in bank or government vaults. Consider the 1881-S Morgan, a coin that the San Francisco Mint struck 12.76 million examples of. As of October 2006, the Professional Coin Grading Service and the Numismatic Guaranty Corporation of America had certified a combined total of 102,306 of these coins as MS-66 and 13,957 as MS-67.

The 1881-S dollar was exceptionally well struck and remains extremely attractive more than a century later. But with so many specimens readily available, is it really worth $350 in MS-66 and $900 in MS-67 (the prices being quoted as this is written)? And does it have good potential to soar in value? Probably not, because many thousands more exist, ready to be certified in equally high grades, increasing the supply even further. This is what is known as a "generic" coin—relatively common even in superb condition. Don't be blinded by the dazzle of this and similar coins.

Some leading coin market analysts, however, take exception to this coin being categorized as a loser. For example, Maurice H. Rosen, editor of an award-winning investment newsletter, calls these coins "speculative favorites" and "great telemarketing coins." Rosen says in his crystal ball, these coins are winners.

The 1864-L Indian Head cent in Extremely Fine condition or better

The Indian Head cent has long been a special favorite with collectors, and in its day it was viewed with great affection by most Americans. Like the Buffalo nickel, it evokes a bygone era when the nation hadn't yet reached full maturity and life was simpler and sweeter—in short, the "good old days." Relations between white settlers and Native American tribes in the West were tumultuous—even downright hostile—during much of the period when this coin was being produced, from 1859 to 1909, but its portrait of a Native American clad in a feather headdress has come to serve as a symbol of our heritage and a tribute to the role that Native Americans played in that panorama.

A quaint, endearing story has persisted through the years that the Indian cent's designer, James Barton Longacre, used his daughter Sarah as his model in preparing the portrait. Supposedly, he sketched it while the young girl posed in a war-bonnet replica. This story gained credence because the "Indian's" features seem more like those of a Caucasian. It now seems unlikely that such a scenario happened; sketches of similar portraits have turned up in Longacre's notebooks from much earlier, indicating a more generic source for his inspiration. But in 1864, five years after the coin's introduction, the artist—then the U.S. Mint's chief engraver—did add a personal touch to the Indian cent: He engraved his initial "L" on the war bonnet's ribbon.

The "L" appears only on bronze Indian cents; copper-nickel specimens from the series' earliest years don't have the designer's initial. And not all bronze cents dated 1864 have the letter, since Longacre didn't add it till late in the year. In fact, collectors have found that 1864 cents with "L" on the ribbon are quite scarce. This has made the coin a coveted collectible, worth hundreds or even thousands of dollars in top condition. Because it is inconspicuous and wears off quickly in circulation, the "L" is readily visible only on coins in at least high circulated grades. The 1864-L Indian Head cent is a legitimate, time-tested rarity with excellent upside potential. At the time of this writing, this coin was retailing for $250 in Extremely Fine condition, a high circulated grade.

Modern proof coins certified in very high grades and sold at ridiculously high prices

Proofs are special coins in more ways than one. Mint technicians choose the very finest planchets (or coin blanks) for proofs; these highly polished blanks are totally free from blemish. They then strike these blanks multiple times with dies that are likewise highly polished. And rather than being tossed in a bin with other newly struck coins, each proof is handled individually and carefully by skilled workmen wearing rubber gloves. All this loving care results in coins with razor-sharp detail, flawless surfaces, and, in many cases, breathtaking cameo contrast between the mirrorlike fields (background areas) and the frosted devices (raised portions bearing the design and the inscriptions).

There isn't any question that proof coins are the ultimate, when viewed from the standpoint of quality. They're head and shoulders above their business-strike cousins—the coins that are produced for use in everyday commerce. And in modern times, particularly since

1968, proofs from the U.S. Mint have been housed in elaborate packaging that shields them quite effectively from mishandling or other damage. Thus, they not only come in pristine condition to begin with, but remain in that exceptional level of preservation far longer than the proofs of previous eras.

It's perfectly understandable that coins with such pizzazz would command a premium. All the extra effort, all the loving care, all the special handling, and all the fancy packaging come at a cost, however, and the Mint is fully justified in passing it along. On the other hand, modern proofs, for all their positive features, have one serious drawback when compared with the proofs of the past: Their quantity, like their quality, is quite high. And unlike high quality, large quantity is a depressant on market value. What's more, their protective packaging keeps these coins in extremely high condition, so even in grades of Proof-67 and above, they're relatively common. Some dealers price them as if they were scarce, but they are decidedly not and you should run, not walk, from any such offering. In fact, NGC founder John Albanese says that although "asking prices are high, it is nearly impossible to find a buyer at any level."

The 1793 Chain and Wreath cents

Early American coppers—the large cents and half cents minted by Uncle Sam in our nation's formative years—enjoy a devoted following in the coin collecting hobby. These pure copper coins represent a link with the earliest days of our nation and the fledgling U.S. Mint and possess a simple charm that transforms mere collecting into a lifelong passion for many of those who pursue them. This attraction is intensified by the availability of seemingly endless varieties of the early coppers, with overdates, small dates, large dates, tall dates, and various permutations of lettering, portraiture, and other design elements keeping collectors constantly on their toes.

The very first U.S. cents, dating from 1793, are among the most intriguing of them all. The Mint launched production in its modest Philadelphia home by issuing a coin that came to be known as the "Chain cent." The obverse of this coin bears a right-facing female head meant to signify Liberty, while the reverse shows the words ONE CENT within a chain of interlocking links. To the Mint's surprise and dismay, the coin encountered hostility from the outset. "The chain on the reverse is but a bad omen for liberty," sniffed one journalist, "and liberty herself appears to be in a fright." People saw the chain not as a symbol of unity, as the Mint intended, but as a suggestion of slavery. The design was quickly replaced by a new one with a modified portrait of Liberty and a wreath on the reverse in place of the chain. Before the year was over, the Wreath cent was gone as well, giving way to a Liberty Cap design.

The Chain cent and Wreath cent are obviously coins of tremendous historical significance. More than that, however, both are major rarities. The Mint produced only about 36,000 Chain cents and 63,000 Wreath cents, and in both cases those mintages are subdivided into several highly collectible varieties. You can expect to pay hundreds of dollars for low-grade specimens of either coin and thousands for high-grade examples, but they're worth it. Seldom in U.S. coinage have history, rarity, and romance intersected so dramatically—and so appealingly.

LOSER
20 ⬇ Bags of uncirculated late-date coins

During the early 1960s, the hottest things on the market were uncirculated rolls of modern U.S. coins: Lincoln cents, Jefferson nickels, Roosevelt dimes, and other contemporary series. The thinking was that if one bright new coin was worth collecting, then a whole roll was 50 times, or 40 times, or 20 times, more desirable and potentially more profitable in the long run. Few stopped to ponder that coins available by the roll probably weren't worth a whole lot to begin with, or that, ultimately, the 50 coins in a roll would have to find their way into 50 different collections in order for their value to be maximized.

Roll collecting fizzled in the mid-1960s when market prices plunged, and nowadays the emphasis is on individual coins in top condition. Some dealers still offer rolls, though, and some collectors, or accumulators, still buy them up and put them away, figuring that their day is bound to come. Carrying this approach to an even greater (and even less logical) extreme, some buy and sell by the bag. In the case of Lincoln cents, there are 5,000 coins—with a total face value of $50—in each bag, and a price exceeding $100 per bag is not uncommon for these uncirculated coins.

Buying bags of coins isn't necessarily a terrible idea. In 1995, for example, some aggressive hobbyists purchased bags of that year's cents in hopes of finding examples of the '95 doubled-die variety—a coin that was then bringing a premium of more than $100. Some struck it rich—in a modest way, at least—by doing just that. Buying bags of silver coins may produce a profit if silver rises in value (assuming that the bags are purchased at minimal markup over their silver value to begin with). But as a general rule, bags should not be bought with an eye to profit potential, especially if that profit is tied to their value as collectibles. True collectors put together sets one coin at a time, not 50, and certainly not 5,000. And without true collectors to give these coins a home, their profit potential is minimal.

The Gobrecht dollar

Although the dollar is the fundamental unit of the U.S. monetary system, there have been long stretches when no dollar coins were produced by the U.S. Mint. One such stretch occurred in the early 19th century. After completing production of 1803 silver dollars in the early part of 1804, the Mint suspended output of this denomination, leaving it on the sidelines for 30 years. Researchers now believe that the rare silver dollars dated 1804 actually came into being in 1834, when the State Department had them struck as gifts for Asian monarchs—choosing the earlier date because it was the last calendar year in which dollar coins had been issued.

The 1804 dollars have a fascinating story all their own. However, they were not the only new dollar coins minted by Uncle Sam in the 1830s. Not long after the diplomatic episode that gave rise to those backdated coins, the Mint began work on an altogether different silver dollar—one with a fresh and dramatic new design. The job of preparing this coin was assigned to Christian Gobrecht, a gifted engraver and medalist who joined the Mint staff in 1835 and later would become its chief engraver. Gobrecht was given designs by two talented artists, Thomas Sully and Titian Peale, and told to use them as the basis for a pair of coinage dies. The stunningly beautiful coin that resulted is known as the Gobrecht dollar.

The Mint struck a series of Gobrecht dollars from 1836 to 1839— some as patterns, others for use in commerce, and all in extremely small numbers. Essentially, these were transitional coins leading up to the start of the Liberty Seated series. In fact, the Gobrecht dollar introduced the Liberty Seated obverse to U.S. coinage. The eagle on its reverse was a bird of a different feather, though, and many critics consider it far superior to the one that perched on Seated coinage of varied denominations for half a century. Gobrecht dollars are rare, beautiful, and distinctive—and if you can afford the typical five-figure price tag, these are great coins to own.

LOSER
21 ⬇

Late-date proof sets from 1968 to date

During the 1950s and early 1960s, collectors looked upon newly is-sued proof sets as a lead-pipe cinch to appreciate in value—and their confidence was justified. During that period, the U.S. Mint offered these sets for $2.10 apiece, and by the time purchasers got their sets from the government in the mail, they inevitably were worth more, and sometimes quite a bit more. Many collectors, and noncollectors, as well, ordered sets in quantities of 10, 20, 50, or even more and sold off the extras within a short time, pocketing the profit. Some put them away as a hedge against inflation, as a nest egg for retirement, or to pay for their children's education.

All this changed in 1968, when the Mint reintroduced proof sets after a three-year lapse caused by a coin shortage during the mid-1960s. The dime and quarter no longer contained precious metal, and the half dollar's silver content was down from 90 percent to only 40 percent. Worse yet, the issue price was more than twice as high; the Mint had raised it from $2.10 per set to $5. In effect, Uncle Sam skimmed off the "guaranteed" profit for himself. Instead of being surefire winners, proof sets became a crapshoot for people who procured them from the Mint. Since that time, they have been a losing proposition on the whole, due, in large part, to numerous price increases that have boosted the issue price considerably. Many of those who purchased single proof sets at issue price from the Mint from 1968 to the present are using red ink in their ledger books (unless the buyer was fortunate enough to get one or more of the very few sets containing mint errors).

While it may appear that proof sets dating back to 1968 would be a bargain today because some are now selling for their issue prices or even less, that is not the case. The supply of many late-date proof sets far exceeds the demand—so unless and until many more collectors are created for this material, the sets are likely to languish for years to come. And the modern proof sets that have increased in value as a result of demand created by the U.S. Mint's State Quarters program will likely see their prices come crashing to earth when the program ends in 2009 or 2010.

The many hundreds of dollars it would cost you for these sets can be spent much more wisely on truly scarce coins.

The 1912-S Liberty Head nickel

The 1913 Liberty Head nickel has one of the highest profiles—and one of the highest values—of any U.S. coin. Only five examples are known, and in 1996 one of them changed hands for close to $1.5 million at the sale of the famous collection of Louis E. Eliasberg Jr. In doing so, it became the first U.S. coin to exceed the million-dollar mark at public auction. As even novice collectors are well aware, however, 1913 Liberty nickels weren't issued officially by the U.S. Mint. In fact, it is believed that all five known examples were struck surreptitiously, and illegally, by a larcenous employee at the Philadelphia Mint who kept them under wraps until he could no longer be punished for this crime by the federal government.

A far less famous and far less valuable—but far more legitimate—rarity occurred in the same nickel series just one year earlier. It will never be a million-dollar coin, but in top mint condition it's worth several thousand. And unlike its 1913 cousin, it's a genuine Mint issue that actually was produced for circulation. The coin in question is the 1912-S Liberty Head nickel—the first U.S. coin of this denomination ever to be struck at the San Francisco Mint.

From 1883, when the Liberty nickel first appeared, through 1911, every coin in this series was minted in Philadelphia. Not until 1912, the final year of the series (at least from the government's perspective), did branch mints get a piece of the action. The Denver Mint produced nearly 8.5 million examples that year, while San Francisco issued just 238,000. Disregarding the 1913, that's easily the lowest mintage in the series—the only one, in fact, below a million. The 1912-S nickel costs upwards of $500 even in grades as low as very fine. It's a coin worth owning in any condition, however, because of its low mintage and its high collector base.

LOSER
22

The 1883 Liberty Head nickel without the word CENTS graded Mint State-65

The Liberty Head nickel is one of the simplest, most straightforward coins ever issued by Uncle Sam. Its design is broad and open, with little subtlety, and its minimal inscriptions are neatly arranged and inconspicuous. The series itself was similarly uncomplicated, for the most part, with hardly any varieties to speak of and branch-mint issues appearing in just one year, 1912—the last official year before this coin gave way to the Buffalo nickel. There was plenty of intrigue at the end of the series, though—with the unofficial striking of the rare 1913 specimens—as well as plenty of excitement at the beginning.

In designing the Liberty nickel, the U.S. Mint's chief engraver, Charles E. Barber, placed a large letter "V" (the Roman numeral representing "5") on the reverse, within a simple wreath. This paralleled the design of the then-current nickel three-cent piece, where the Roman numeral III was on the reverse. Barber saw no need to add the word CENTS; after all, it didn't appear on the three-cent piece. Soon after the nickel first hit circulation, though, crafty con men began to gold-plate it and pass it off on unsuspecting merchants as a new $5 gold piece. They were aided in this chicanery by the absence of the crucial word CENTS. Barber hastily prepared a new reverse design incorporating that word, and this, along with word of mouth, resolved the problem.

Production of Liberty nickels in 1883 included both varieties; by year's end, the Mint had struck a total of about 21.5 million of the new nickels, and nearly three-fourths of them—more than 16 million—had the word CENTS on the reverse. Mintage of the no-CENTS variety, having been halted early in the year, totaled less than 5.5 million. But people set aside the earlier variety in substantially greater numbers than the later one, reasoning that because it had been replaced, it would bring a handsome premium down the line. In fact, just the opposite has occurred: The second variety, with the word CENTS, is much scarcer today in pristine mint condition because it wasn't saved to nearly the same extent. The no-CENTS nickel, on the other hand, is the lowest-priced coin in the entire series in MS-65, currently bringing about $350 in that grade. Even at that price, I would avoid it. Just too many mint-fresh examples were saved, and too many still exist.

WINNER

23 ⬆

The 1937-D three-legged Buffalo nickel

Freak accidents can cause major financial hardship, not to mention injury or death, when they happen on the highway. They can lead to a bonanza, though, when they happen in the press room at one of the U.S. mints. Consider the case of the "three-legged" Buffalo nickel. This fascinating mint-error coin, now a popular variety worth hundreds—even thousands—of dollars, came into being because a Mint workman failed to clean up properly after such an accident.

A coin is produced when a planchet (or coin blank) is stamped simultaneously by two dies—one imparting the obverse design, the other the reverse. Occasionally, the machinery jams and fails to feed a planchet into position. When that happens, the dies strike each

other instead and each incurs damage from the other. These damaged dies are said to have "clash marks," and standard procedure
calls for stopping the press and removing them from service. But on
one such occasion in 1937, a workman at the Denver Mint decided to
take a shortcut: Instead of replacing the dies, he pulled out an emery
stick and ground off the clash marks on a Buffalo nickel die. He may
not have noticed it at first, but this removed not only the unwanted
marks but also much of the foreleg of the bison on the die for the
coin's reverse. Significant numbers of nickels were struck with this
defect and escaped into circulation before the problem was spotted
and corrected.

No one knows for sure exactly how many "three-legged" 1937-D
nickels got out. The figure is believed to be relatively modest, however. And over the years, this "accidental" coin has caught collectors'
fancy and become a widely recognized and much desired part of the
Buffalo series. It will cost you more than $1,000 even in the lowly
grade of good, and more than $2,750 in mint condition. The cost is
justified, though, for while this coin may be a freak, it's legitimately
scarce and perennially popular with a broad range of collectors.

Mint-error coins where significant magnification is needed to see the mistake

Mint errors have become increasingly popular with collectors in recent years. Major mistakes have always enjoyed a following and always commanded a premium. The three-legged Buffalo nickel
attests to this, as do such overdate coins as the 1918-over-17-D Buffalo nickel, the 1918-over-17-S Standing Liberty quarter, and the
1942-over-1 Mercury dime. All of these are viewed not only as im-

portant varieties but also as desirable—and valuable—rarities. But over the last three decades or so, error-coin collecting has expanded from a fascinating specialty with a relatively modest but enthusiastic following into one of the biggest growth areas in the hobby. And its devotees are looking for ever-less-conspicuous minting mistakes.

This is undoubtedly due in part to the fact that scarce-date coins, precious-metal issues, and other coins with premium value are so much harder to find today in ordinary pocket change. A generation ago, collectors could go to the bank, pick up a few dozen rolls of cents, nickels, or other current coins, take them home, examine them, and turn up quite a few that were worth at least a modest amount above face. Today, they have to look harder and closer to find collectible coins: Instead of seeking coins with scarce dates or valuable date-and-mint combinations, they look for coins with interesting and potentially scarce imperfections. This kind of searching paid off in 1995, when sharp-eyed collectors found noticeable doubling on some of that year's cents from the Philadelphia Mint. Those coins turned out to be more common than first believed, but they still bring a decent premium.

To mint-error specialists, even small mistakes can be highly appealing. You should be wary, however, of paying a big premium for a mint error so small that it needs to be examined under a magnifying glass in order to be seen and appreciated. Size does count in this instance. As a general rule, the bigger and more obvious the mistake, the greater the premium value.

The two-cent piece in Mint State-65 Red

The two-cent piece was one of the shortest-lived coins in U.S. history, lasting barely 10 years before it was consigned to the burial ground for dead denominations. It left an enduring legacy, though, for while it failed to carve a niche for itself in circulation, it will always be remembered as the coin that introduced the now-familiar motto IN GOD WE TRUST.

This large bronze coin was very much a product of its time—and specifically a result of the Civil War. Two separate war-related influences combined to bring it about. One was the almost total disappearance of existing U.S. coinage during the first few years of that epic conflict: Hoarding became a national obsession, with gold and silver coins vanishing from circulation first, followed soon afterward by copper and copper-nickel issues. Observing the wide acceptance of privately issued small bronze tokens as emergency wartime money, the Treasury decided in 1864 to slenderize the Indian Head cent and change its composition from copper-nickel to bronze. At the same time, it introduced a larger bronze companion, the two-cent piece, to help reinforce the beachhead it was seeking to establish for new coins in circulation. Meanwhile, religious fervor, kindled by the agonies of the war, gave rise to sentiment for recognizing God on the nation's coinage, and the two-cent piece was chosen to serve as a showcase for that tribute.

Initially, two-cent pieces circulated widely, filling the coinage void as they were intended to do. Within a few years, though, the public began to shun them as older coins reappeared and newer, more convenient alternatives were produced in the postwar years. Mintage shrunk from nearly 20 million in 1864 to only 65,000 in 1872. Only proofs were issued in 1873, and after that the series was laid to rest. Because of the high usage of early two-cent pieces and the low mintage of later ones, relatively few exist today in pristine mint condition. Even among the ones that were saved initially, many were mishandled over the years. In Mint State-65, common-date examples cost $1,300 or more today—but the price is right, because these are truly scarce, historic coins.

Proof coins priced excessively high because their business-strike counterparts are scarce

We've all heard the expression that you can't compare apples and oranges. Yet, now and then, people who buy and sell coins do just that. They do it when they assign an inordinately high value to a proof coin just because the regular-quality coin of the same type and date—the business-strike version—is scarce and commands a premium above the market value of common-date issues. The business strike here is the apple and the proof is the orange, and just because the apple is exceptionally tasty and desirable, it doesn't make the orange any juicier.

Consider the case of the 1877 Indian Head cent. This has long been regarded as the single biggest "key" in the Indian series. It's one of only two Indian cents with mintages below a million—and while the other coin (the 1909-S) was made in smaller numbers, the 1877 is worth more across the board, in every single grade, because it was saved in far smaller quantities and distributed much more widely. But what we're referring to here is the "apple" factor—the business-strike mintage of the coin. At 852,500, it's exceptionally scarce by the standards of cent collecting, and the high ongoing demand justifies the premium this coin has always brought. The U.S. Mint also produced about 900 proof cents in 1877. While that is surely a modest figure, it's higher than the proof mintage of the 1874 Indian cent, of which only about 700 were struck. Yet the 1877 is valued at five times as much in Proof-65 Red—$15,000, compared with $3,000 for other dates, such as the 1874.

Clearly, this is a case in which the value of the apple has inflated the price tag of the orange. There is no evidence that proof 1877 cents have suffered a higher attrition rate than the two earlier proofs. If anything, those should be worth more since they have lower mintages. In short, proofs should be compared with proofs, regardless of the corresponding business-strike mintages. Some spillover effect is inevitable, but a fourfold higher premium is excessive.

Shield nickels graded Proof-65 or higher

In recent years, Americans have gotten by with only four truly circulating coins: the cent, nickel, dime, and quarter. The U.S. Mint produces half dollars for circulation, but they see little actual use. Be-ginning in 1999, the U.S. Mint struck a dollar coin for use in daily commerce, but it was not widely circulated. Conditions were far dif-ferent in the 19th century, when the Mint routinely made upwards of a dozen different coins for circulation, including at times two kinds with the same face value.

Five-cent pieces were one example of duplication. Right from the start of U.S. federal coinage in the early 1790s, the Mint had pro-duced a small silver coin called the half dime, which, as its name suggests, weighed exactly half as much as the dime. In 1865, with gold and silver coins still among the missing because of Civil War hoarding, the Mint decided to strike a copper-nickel five-cent piece as a means to help retire the fractional five-cent notes issued by the government on an emergency basis during the war. The new coin made its debut in 1866 and came to be known as the Shield nickel because of the ornate shield shown on its obverse.

A case can be made that the Shield nickel was one of the ugliest coins in U.S. history. It certainly was one of the least aesthetic, with the uninspiring shield on one side and the simple number "5" on the re-verse. Whatever its shortcomings, it did establish the copper-nickel five-cent piece, or "nickel," as a useful, popular coin. And over the years, it has gained favor with many collectors—not because of its appearance but because of the genuine scarcity of many dates in the series. Shield nickels were minted for 17 years, and in only three of those years did production exceed 10 million. Proofs were produced every year, and their mintages were generally very low—less than 1,000 in many cases. Even a "common-date" Proof-65 example will cost you close to $600, but at the market's high in 1989 that same coin would have cost $2,500. To me, it's a wonderful value at today's price and has tremendous potential.

LOSER
25

Common-date Peace dollars graded Mint State-63 and 64

The Great War (later renamed World War I) decimated the male populations of Britain, France, Germany, and Austria-Hungary and also claimed the lives of more than 50,000 American "Doughboys." It was optimistically labeled "The War to End All Wars," and after the declaration of an armistice on November 11, 1918, high-minded leaders and individual citizens the world over set out to ensure that such a conflagration would never happen again. To that end, they set up the League of Nations, hoping that a world body dedicated to peace would serve as a firewall against any future war. Sadly, of course, the League—and that hope—would be in vain.

The League of Nations' failure stemmed in large measure from Uncle Sam's abandonment of the idealistic venture. Instead of joining the League, the United States retreated into a shell of isolationism, unwittingly helping thereby to sow the bitter seeds of an even more devastating conflict. The yearning for a lasting peace did give rise to tangible expressions of Americans' sentiment, though, one of which took the form of a handsome new coin. The coin, a silver dollar, quickly came to be known as the "Peace dollar" because—alone among circulating U.S. coinage—it has the word PEACE as an inscription.

The Peace dollar had a short life span, from 1921 to 1935, and wasn't minted at all from 1929 through 1933, largely because of diminished need for coinage at the onset of the Great Depression. It tends to be weakly struck, and any imperfections are magnified by its broad, open design. As a consequence, it's quite scarce in the higher-end grades of Mint State-65 and above. At the same time, it exists in relatively high numbers in the mid-range grades of Mint State-63 and 64, especially in the case of common-date issues. A large supply translates into lower market value and serves as a depressant on future potential. That's a yellow warning light for you, the consumer: This is not the best road to go down.

WINNER
26 ⬆

The 1926-S Lincoln cent graded Mint State-64 Red

Collectors with a taste for Lincoln cents have long recognized the 1926-S as one of the scarcer coins in the series but have tended to relegate it to the status of a "semi-key"—very desirable but not on a par with such lower-mintage issues as the 1909-S VDB, 1909-S, and 1914-D. Based on mintage alone, this assessment is not unreasonable, and it seems perfectly logical that for many years, the '26-S carried lower valuations than a number of other early Lincolns in popular price guides.

That situation still holds true today in circulated and lower Mint State grades. But in higher Mint State grades, a dramatic change has occurred: In searching for pristine specimens of various Lincoln cents, hobbyists have discovered that the 1926-S is far more elusive than its mintage of just over 4.5 million would suggest. It is, in fact, the single most difficult Lincoln to obtain in the grade of MS-65 Red. And this is now reflected in its price: In that exceptional grade, the '26-S cent currently carries a premium of more than $100,000.

To me, that price is simply too high, despite the great rarity of MS-65 Red examples of this coin. But I strongly recommend '26-S cents in the next-highest grade—MS-64 Red—because they sell for only one-tenth as much, about $10,000, and aren't much more available than 65 Red examples.

Sharply struck specimens of high-grade Lincoln cents and other denominations exist in very small numbers for dates throughout the 1920s. One theory is that the U.S. Mint was on an economy kick at the time and used dies beyond their normal life span, especially at the two branch mints in Denver and San Francisco. That would help account for the disproportionate number of weakly struck coins. It also has been suggested that the Mint may have increased the space between dies, reducing die wear but also resulting in many weak strikes.

For whatever reason, the problem came to a head in 1926, when weak strikes were rampant and sharply struck coins were almost impossible to find. Buffalo nickels had their lowest mintage ever that year, which, combined with the preponderance of weak strikes, drove demand for sharp, high-grade '26-S nickels to the point at which they, too, now sell for more than $100,000 in MS-65 condition. In yet another parallel with '26-S cents, these nickels bring big but much more reasonable premiums—about $16,000 at this writing—in the grade of MS-64.

The '26-S cent isn't the lowest-mintage Lincoln, but its mintage does rank among the 10 lowest in the series (not counting errors and varieties). And because of its many weak strikes, high-grade pieces with even decent strikes command bonus prices way out of proportion to the mintage. At a time when MS-64 Red examples of the '26-S Red cent are selling for $10,000 or more, similar specimens of the 1909-S VDB cent—a coin with a mintage almost 10 times smaller—are available for only $8,500.

Any way you look at it, the '26-S cent is a winner in MS-64 Red. It's a worthy companion to the '26-S Buffalo nickel in that grade.

LOSER
26 ⬇

Picked-through rolls of uncirculated silver dollars

"Originality counts." Those words are often heard in contests calling for entries of 25 words or less. Originality counts with collectible coins, as well: Dealers and collectors place a premium—often a high one—on coins with original luster, sets in original holders, and rolls that were assembled from the same original bag of mint-fresh coins. Being "original" translates into being free from tarnish, taint, or tampering.

A generation ago, it was relatively easy to obtain an original roll—or, for that matter, a full original bag—of Morgan or Peace silver dollars. "Cartwheels" hadn't yet emerged as special favorites of investment-minded buyers; they were playing second fiddle to smaller, more modern coins in the marketplace of the early 1960s. A roll of common-date Morgans in BU (brilliant uncirculated) condition could be acquired then for about the same price as a single such coin today. And, more often than not, that roll would be original—just the way it came from an old-time bag, with all 20 coins matched closely in quality and appearance.

Over the years, the market changed dramatically. Modern coins lost favor and gained favor, silver bullion rose in value sharply, and silver dollars came to be the darlings of a new breed of coin collector/investor. With these changes came heavy new emphasis on the quality of coins, or their level of preservation. And that, in turn, led people with rolls and bags of coins, especially silver dollars, to scrutinize each coin and pull out any specimens with a little extra pizzazz because even slight differences in luster, sharpness, or toning could mean a substantial difference in market value. This process was repeated time and again, to the point where truly original rolls are few and far between. You'll see BU dollar rolls offered for sale at shows, and the current wholesale price of $550 ($27.70 per coin) for common-date issues may seem attractive. Keep in mind, however, that you'll be getting sludge. The nice coins will be gone, and you'll be getting dregs no one else wanted. The upside to these coins is that they will increase in value if silver increases in value ($11.50 per ounce in October 2006). There are better ways, however, to capitalize on silver's value soaring than these off-grade coins.

Draped Bust silver dollars and half dollars graded AU-50 to AU-55

A dollar was big money in early America. Although the Founding Fathers established it as the cornerstone of the U.S. monetary system, it was too high an amount to be practical in the form of a single coin. As a result, silver dollars were minted sparingly, and in very small quantities, during the first decade or so of U.S. coinage—and not at all thereafter for more than 30 years. For all intents and purposes, the half dollar was the highest-value coin encountered in everyday commerce by most Americans.

Design changes were frequent in early U.S. coinage, and the silver dollar and half dollar both underwent several major revisions during the first few years of their existence. The very first coins of both denominations carried a "Flowing Hair" portrait of Miss Liberty, but this was soon discarded in favor of a more sedate—and decidedly more mature—likeness commonly referred to as the "Draped Bust" type. This made its debut on the dollar in 1795 and was placed on the half dollar the following year. It shows Miss Liberty facing to the right with a ribbon in her hair and drapery covering much, but not all, of her rather ample bosom. At first, the reverse of the Flowing Hair design, depicting a small eagle, was retained on the reverse of the Draped Bust type, but later this gave way to an eagle with a shield upon its breast—an eagle that is said to be "heraldic."

The most famous Draped Bust dollar—the 1804—is a story in itself and ranks among the most valuable of all U.S. coins. Few can hope to own this great rarity, but the earlier coins in the series, from 1795 to 1803, while attainable, are also far from inexpensive; they all have mintages under half a million and, in most cases, under 100,000. Draped Bust half dollars lingered until 1807, but topped 500,000 in just one year, 1806. Both denominations are prohibitively expensive in mint condition. They'll set you back several thousand dollars even in about uncirculated (AU) condition, but as rare, historic, and highly coveted coins, they're well worth the outlay.

LOSER

27 ⬇

Russian 5-ruble gold coins certified in grades of Mint State-65 and above and sold for excessively high prices

Certification of rare coins by independent third-party grading services has been a boon to the market in recent years, greatly reducing contentiousness over coins' level of preservation and giving buyers and sellers a heightened sense of confidence. Certification of common coins has led to abuses, however, and one of the prime examples is the extensive promotion and sale of Russian 5-ruble gold coins from the turn of the 20th century at highly inflated prices because they've been certified in high mint-state grades.

The coins being offered are interesting from a historic standpoint; they carry the portrait of Nicholas II, last of the czars, who, along with the rest of the royal family, died at the hands of a firing squad following the Russian Revolution. They also contain precious metal: not quite one-fifth of an ounce of gold, or slightly less than a U.S. half eagle ($5 gold piece). And, as the grades assigned to them attest, they're in a high level of preservation. But the prices being charged by unscrupulous promoters are far above the coins' actual market value.

To begin with, 5-ruble coins of Nicholas II were made in tremendous quantities. Some dates are scarce, to be sure, but others were produced in massive numbers; the 1898, for example, had a mintage of more than 52 million. And many pieces were saved in mint condition by the czar and later by Soviet authorities—stored in Swiss bank vaults very much the way that Morgan silver dollars remained in Treasury vaults in this country. As a result, these coins are readily available in mint condition, even in grades as high as Mint State-66 or 67. And whereas Morgan dollars are widely collected by date and coveted in high grades, most collectors acquire the Russian 5-ruble, if at all, as a type coin and won't pay more than a nominal premium for high quality. As this is written, the 5-ruble coin contains less than $140 worth of gold at the current bullion value of $620 per ounce, yet some promoters are selling it for more than double that. To me, that's a rip-off.

Early $2½, $5, and $10 gold pieces in EF and AU condition

Gold has not been part of America's circulating coinage since 1933, and it saw little actual use in the nation's daily commerce even then. The Founding Fathers felt deeply, however, that issuing gold coins was an important means of lending credibility and prestige to U.S. coinage—and to the nation itself—when the United States first took its place on the world stage, and the practice continued for nearly a century and a half. Not until the Great Depression ravaged the nation's economy did Uncle Sam retreat from this commitment.

The Mint Act of 1792 provided for the issuance of three gold coins: an eagle, or $10 gold piece; a half eagle ($5); and a quarter eagle ($2½). The eagle and half eagle made their first appearance in 1795, with the quarter eagle joining them in 1796. Other denominations, most notably the double eagle (or $20 gold piece), came along later, after the discovery of gold in California. But these three coins collectively formed the cornerstone of U.S. gold coinage, and they were the only ones produced before 1849.

When we refer to early U.S. gold coins, we really place the dividing line not in 1849, but rather a decade earlier. It was in 1838 that the U.S. Mint introduced the Coronet design on gold coinage, and because this design persisted until 1908, it is usually associated with a more mature period of the Mint's history. In the early period, the eagle was produced only from 1795 to 1804 and came with a Capped Bust portrait of Miss Liberty. The half eagle was issued almost every year, but the quarter eagle appeared somewhat sporadically, and not at all from 1809 through 1820. Both went through a series of design changes, evolving from the early Capped Bust facing right to a different Capped Bust facing left, then to a Capped Head version, and finally to the so-called Classic Head. All of these are charming, most have extremely low mintages, and all are highly desirable. You'll pay thousands of dollars for one of these coins, even in EF or AU condition, but you'll have a solid collectible that's also an excellent investment.

LOSER
28 ⬇ Common-date British sovereigns in mint condition sold for excessively high prices

The British sovereign is one of the best known and most historic gold coins in the world. First issued in 1489, it has remained in production for centuries, right into modern times, and has attained a high degree of recognition and use in many parts of the world. Its acceptance is so universal, in fact, that during World War II the survival kits issued to Allied fliers—intended for use if they were shot down in unfamiliar territory—included examples of this coin. Most sovereigns struck since 1817 have carried a portrait of St. George slaying a dragon, and this design, one of the most familiar in coinage history, has reinforced the coin's popularity and ready recognition.

Sovereigns have been produced not only by the British Royal Mint, but also by mints in far-flung outposts of the British Empire, and some of these coins are quite scarce and even rare. Many other sovereigns were struck by the millions, however, and are worth just a nominal premium over the market value of the metal they contain, which is slightly less than one-fourth of an ounce of gold. In effect, they are little more than bullion-type coins.

In recent years, fast-buck artists have found a way to reap big profits from these small-premium coins. They buy up common-date sovereigns in a high level of preservation—coins that are readily available in substantial quantities—and submit them to one of the third-party certification services. Then, when the coins are encapsulated with grades of, say, Mint State-65 or 66, they offer them for sale at greatly inflated prices as if they were rare and numismatically valuable in those grades. "There are tons of this stuff around," says respected hobby researcher R.W. Julian, "and it simply isn't worth a huge premium. A small premium, yes, but that's all." With gold bullion selling for $620 per ounce, a fair market price might be $200. If someone is charging much more, he or she is trying to rip you off.

Seated Liberty dollars graded AU-50 to AU-55

U.S. coin designs underwent frequent changes during the nation's formative years. The U.S. Mint seemed to be constantly tinkering with the images it presented to the world through the medium of legal-tender coinage. Miss Liberty appeared with flowing hair, a cap, a draped bust, a capped bust, a capped head, a Classic head, facing right, facing left—all in the first four decades of federal coinage. It is quite a contrast with the sameness of the nation's modern coinage, where design changes occur, if at all, at a glacial pace. Seemingly endless die varieties compounded the remarkable diversity.

By the mid-1830s, the nation had achieved a measure of maturity and stability, and it was time for U.S. coinage to do the same. Robert Maskell Patterson accelerated the process when he became Mint director in 1835. Patterson wanted to upgrade U.S. coin designs to put them on a par with those of Europe, and, with that in mind, he oversaw creation of a stunning new silver dollar by engraver Christian Gobrecht. This coin, first struck in 1836, served as the prototype for the Seated Liberty coinage, which remained in use for more than half a century.

Oddly, the dollar was the last silver coin to bear the permanent version of the Seated Liberty portraiture—the one that paired Miss Liberty with a heraldic eagle. The first silver dollar to carry this design didn't appear on the scene until 1840. And though it was produced on a regular annual basis until it was discontinued in 1873, mintages were modest for the most part, exceeding 1 million (and doing so barely, at that) only in 1871 and 1872. Mintages below 100,000—and even below 10,000—were far more typical. As you might expect, these coins bring a pretty penny—thousands of dollars, in fact—in choice mint condition. High-grade circulated examples—certified as, say, About Uncirculated-50 or AU-55—can be had for just a few hundred dollars, and while they may lack the sizzle of an MS-65 piece, they still give you plenty of "steak": scarce, historic coins in desirable, collectible condition.

Big-mintage modern commemorative coins from small, obscure countries

Of all the "losers" profiled in this book, there probably isn't a single one with more dismal investment potential than modern commemorative coins from obscure countries, including some issuers that may not be countries at all. They range all the way from base-metal coins priced at less than $10 apiece to gold and platinum coins costing hundreds of dollars each or and possibly even thousands. But they have three things in common: issue prices far above the intrinsic worth of their metal, virtually no collector base, and absolutely zero upside potential to ever rise in value above what they'd bring as bullion.

Chances are you've seen commercials on TV, or ads in the paper, for coins from the Marshall Islands tied to some major event in the news or some noteworthy anniversary. We saw this sort of thing when Britain's Princess Diana was killed, for example, and on the 25th anniversary of the *Apollo 11* moon landing. The events certainly merited commemorative coinage, and if there had been a British coin at the time to honor Princess Di, or a U.S. coin for the moon landing, they would have been prime collectibles. But Marshall Islands "coins" are really nothing but overpriced tokens and medals, and hardly anyone collects them, unlike British and U.S. coins. The only ones who profit are the Marshall Islands themselves and the people who are promoting this tawdry trash.

You also should steer clear of the many new coins from the Isle of Man. These may have a bit more respectability than Marshall Islands issues, but they have about the same investment potential: the potential of a heat wave in Antarctica.

WINNER

30

Copper-nickel Indian Head cents graded Mint State-64

The first small-size U.S. one-cent piece, the Flying Eagle cent, was popular with most Americans. By 1857, when this coin made its debut in circulation, people had grown tired of lugging around the pure copper "large cent." While they may not have referred to it by that term, its bulky size (not much smaller or lighter than our present-day half dollar) was weighing down, and wearing holes in, many pockets. The Flying Eagle cent, though popular, had a fatal flaw: It was prone to weakness of strike because the high points on its obverse were opposite the high points on its reverse. The U.S. Mint's chief engraver, James B. Longacre, was directed to come up with a new design.

Longacre, who also designed the Flying Eagle cent, scored an even bigger hit with its replacement, for the coin he fashioned next—the Indian Head cent—went on to become one of this nation's most familiar and most admired. It remained in production for fully half a century before giving way to the even longer-running Lincoln cent in 1909.

Initially, the Indian cent had the same specifications as the Flying Eagle. It was the same diameter as today's Lincoln cent but, at 4.67 grams, it weighed nearly twice as much. And it was struck from an alloy of 88 percent copper and 12 percent nickel, which gave it a light tan appearance and led some people to refer to it as a "white cent." After only two full years of production, however, it was caught up in the coin hoarding sparked by the Civil War and virtually disappeared from circulation. In 1864, the Mint introduced a slenderized Indian cent made of bronze and thereby reestablished a beachhead in commerce for the coin. The copper-nickel version had been minted in only six years: 1859 through the first part of 1864. Although its annual mintages weren't small by the standards of the day, ranging between 10 million and 50 million, this "white" Indian cent enjoys wide popularity as a type coin. In Mint State-64, it costs about $300 (not counting the higher-priced 1859), but I consider that a good value.

LOSER

30 ⬇ "Double-trouble" coins

There's a certain amount of guesswork, and risk, involved in trying to figure out what kind of grade an uncertified (or "raw") coin will receive when it's submitted to one of the third-party grading services. The risk can be substantial because small variations in the grade of a coin sometimes result in very large differences in that coin's market value. Further risk would seem to be eliminated once the coin is certified and encapsulated because presumably it can be sold at that point for the value corresponding to the grade it has been assigned. But that's not necessarily true for all time and in each and every case. Experts can distinguish a "just-made-it" coin graded Mint State-65 from one that nearly qualifies for Mint State-66, for example, and they naturally have a preference—and perhaps a higher buying price—for premium-quality coins.

The risk is compounded, as is the potential for erosion of your investment, when a coin has a special characteristic incorporated into its grade and, by extension, its market value. That's what happens with Morgan silver dollars that are classified as having Deep-Mirror Prooflike (DMPL) surfaces, or Mercury dimes with Full Split Bands on the fasces on the reverse, or Franklin half dollars with Full Bell Lines on the Liberty Bell. These qualities enhance the appeal and the value of these coins, but at the same time, they open another front in the ongoing long-term battle over just what the coins are really worth.

I refer to these as "double-trouble" coins. The very characteristics that seem positive at the outset can have negative implications in the long run if a disagreement develops over the grading—as can and does happen even with certified coins—or if the coins at some point are removed from their grading-service holders. It's hard enough to get a consensus concerning the grade of a coin; it's doubly difficult to get complete agreement on a second point, such as whether the bell lines are really full. That gives people *two* things to disagree about, and that's double jeopardy.

Proof-65 Mercury dimes

The "Mercury dime" is widely acclaimed as one of the most beautiful of all U.S. coins. It's also one of the most misunderstood. Soon after this lovely coin made its appearance in 1916, many Americans came to the conclusion that the figure portrayed on its obverse must be Mercury, the messenger of the gods in Roman mythology, because of the winged cap "he" wore. In fact, the figure is female—a classical depiction of Miss Liberty—and the coin's designer, sculptor Adolph A. Weinman, intended her wings to symbolize "liberty of thought." Although the misnomer "Mercury dime" has stuck to this coin ever since, its proper appellation is the Winged Liberty Head, or simply Winged Liberty, dime.

Just as a rose by any other name would smell as sweet, the Winged Liberty dime remains a magnificent coin no matter how inaccurately it may be described. The amazing thing about its aesthetic brilliance is that the artist achieved this despite having such a tiny "canvas" to work with. The modern U.S. dime is just 17.9 millimeters—less than three-quarters of an inch—in diameter, so this coin is truly a miniature masterpiece. The fasces, the Roman symbol of authority depicted on its reverse, later became associated with Italian dictator Benito Mussolini, but this can hardly be held against Weinman or the remarkable coin he designed.

The beauty of any coin can be seen to maximum advantage on proof examples. Unfortunately, the U.S. Mint was not producing annual proofs during much of the lifetime of the Winged Liberty dime, from 1916 to 1945. It did make them, though, for seven of the 30 years in which the coin was issued—from 1936 through 1942. The proofs from the 1930s all have mintages below 10,000 and tend to be more expensive than the later issues, especially in the case of the 1936. Those from 1940 through 1942 have slightly higher mintages but are still scarce, and they can be acquired in Proof-65 for not much more than $300 apiece—about one-fifth what they were bringing in 1989. Truly, these are beautiful investments.

LOSER
31 ⬇ A roll of common-date Mercury dimes in average uncirculated condition

It's hard to imagine today, but not so many years ago buying modern coins by the roll was a major preoccupation of many, if not most, buyers and sellers. In the superheated market of the early 1960s, so-called collectors competed tooth and nail for the right to acquire such prizes as 50-piece rolls of 1955-S Lincoln cents (at about $1 per coin) and 40-piece rolls of 1950-D Jefferson nickels (at up to $30 per coin). In some respects, this was not unlike a Ponzi scheme because the only way most late-date cents and nickels could hold or increase those values was for new buyers to enter the market in increments of 50 for each available cent roll and 40 for each nickel roll. Clearly, that was not about to happen.

Not all coin rolls offered for sale at that time were bad investments, however. Sprinkled among the ads for late-date Lincoln cent and Jefferson nickel rolls were offerings of uncirculated rolls, or possibly half-rolls, of somewhat earlier coins, such as Buffalo nickels, Winged Liberty ("Mercury") dimes, and Walking Liberty half dollars. And while the dates being offered were almost always common ones in those series, these coins—unlike later-date Lincolns and Jeffersons—hadn't been set aside in uncirculated condition to nearly the same extent. As a result, they're worth much more today than they were in the early 1960s.

Rolls of these coins, especially Mercury dimes from the later years of that series, are advertised occasionally today. Typically, they are priced at hundreds of dollars per roll. Chances are that this time, these coins are poor investments. First and foremost, the premium value of high-quality coins is so much greater today that these rolls almost certainly have been picked over. You'll be lucky to find anything that's better than Mint State-60 or 61. Beyond that, buyers today favor individual coins in choice condition. The last thing they want is a roll of coins in less than top shape.

Common-date Barber silver coins in Mint State-64 or 65, or Proof-64 or 65

Charles E. Barber was the U.S. Mint's chief sculptor-engraver for nearly four decades, from 1879 to 1917—longer by far than any other occupant of that job. During that time, he had a hand in designing a number of new coins, including the Liberty Head nickel, the flowing-hair Stella (or $4 gold piece), the Columbian half dollar (the nation's very first commemorative coin), and several other silver and gold commemoratives. Some would say he also had a hand in sabotaging other designers' work; he has been widely criticized for reducing the relief overzealously on Augustus Saint-Gaudens's double eagle and James Earl Fraser's Buffalo nickel. Of all Barber's coinage accomplishments, none is identified more closely with him—or represents a finer legacy—than the turn-of-the-century half dollar, quarter, and dime.

Throughout the first century of U.S. coinage, the half dollar, quarter, and dime—joined for long stretches by the silver dollar and half dime—had been uniform in design at any given time. Barber continued this practice with his lookalike designs for the three new silver coins of 1892. Each depicts the head of Miss Liberty on the obverse, facing right, and the half dollar and quarter also share a common heraldic-eagle portrait on the reverse. Being too small for the eagle, the dime's reverse bears only the words ONE DIME within a wreath. These coins may not have been soaring works of art, but they were well-suited symbolically for the period when they were issued, from 1892 through 1916. And they wore extremely well, circulating all the way into the 1950s.

Unlike Morgan dollars, which saw only limited use, the Barber coins served Americans long and well in commerce, and relatively few were preserved in mint condition. As a result, they're elusive in high mint-state grades. You can expect to pay hundreds of dollars for even a common-date example in Mint State-64 or 65 and more for a Proof-64 or 65, as proof mintages rarely exceeded 1,000. But these coins are legitimately scarce and the prices are justified.

A complete set of average uncirculated Franklin half dollars

The Franklin half dollar is a coin with a pleasing appearance whose broad, open design features two of the most admired icons from this nation's Revolutionary period: Benjamin Franklin and the Liberty Bell. It was issued for a relatively brief span—from 1948 through 1963—before giving way to the Kennedy half dollar in the traumatic days following the assassination of President John F. Kennedy. It has only 35 date-and-mint varieties, and its lowest-mintage coin, the 1953, isn't terribly scarce at a figure of nearly 2.8 million. It has the distinction of being the last circulating U.S. coin struck entirely in silver, or rather, the traditional U.S. coinage alloy of 90 percent silver and 10 percent copper.

Given all this, you might assume that assembling a set of Franklin half dollars in attractive mint condition would be easy and inexpensive. After all, this is a modern coin that presumably was saved in significant quantities by the roll, or even the bag, when it was new. And you would be correct—to a point. Many Franklin halves were preserved in mint condition and can be obtained today for modest premiums. But few Franklin halves existed to begin with in extremely high condition with sharp strikes and fully defined details. And those coins today bring, and deserve to bring, very high premiums, while typical BU Franklins are cheap and deservedly so.

The *Coin Dealer Newsletter* (or *Greysheet*) shows a bid price, at this writing, of $525 for a set of uncirculated Franklin half dollars. This corresponds to a set in which the coins average Mint State-63. That may seem inexpensive, but it really isn't a bargain, since Franklins in that grade are generally quite common. What's more, there's a hidden danger: Often, the common dates will be nice BU coins but the key dates, such as the 1949-D and S, will be sliders. The set will look appealing as a whole, but the coins that should represent most of the value won't be worth much of a premium because they aren't really uncirculated. That's a double whammy.

WINNER

33

Twenty-cent pieces certified as Proof-63 or 64

The 20-cent piece may have been the most unnecessary coin in U.S. history. It certainly was one of the most unsuccessful: It was struck for circulation for only two years before being reduced to a proof-only issue. Then, after just two more years on that life-support status, it limped into the sunset. Yet, in a sense, this odd silver coin went to heaven when it died, for it has enjoyed a highly successful afterlife as a collectible.

There was no real reason to issue such a coin, at least from the perspective of the American public. But Western silver miners were awash in precious metal at the time the coin was authorized in 1875. Nevada's Comstock Lode had done for silver mining what Sutter's Mill had done for gold mining 25 years earlier—and yet, with all this silver pouring into the marketplace, the Mint Act of 1873 had removed a major outlet by halting further production of silver dollars. Outraged silver miners and their friends on Capitol Hill soon began seeking new coinage uses for the metal; one of the dividends, from the miners' point of view, was the 20-cent piece.

Aside from serving no useful purpose not accomplished already by two dimes, the 20-cent piece suffered from bad design work. It looked much the same as the Seated Liberty quarter, and since it was the same composition and close to the same size, people confused the two coins. The eagle on its reverse faced the other way and the edge of the coin was smooth, rather than reeded (as on the quarter), but these were subtle differences, and in the big picture the coins were too close in appearance. In 1878, the silver interests got a new dollar coin and last rites were held for the 20-cent piece. Its rebirth as a collectible stems not from its short lifespan, but rather from its very low mintages. You'll pay about $2,300 in Proof-63 and $4,000 in Proof-64. But when it comes to investment, these coins have lots of life in them.

LOSER

33 ⬇ Oversized replicas of U.S. coins struck privately in silver

They say that big is beautiful. And that may be true, but it isn't when it comes to coins. Advertisers use this idea to hype the bigness—and the beauty—of oversized silver "collectibles" that are based all too closely on genuine U.S. coins (and sometimes on U.S. paper money). The strong suggestion here is that the collectibility, legitimacy, and investment potential of the actual U.S. coins somehow rub off on these hefty replicas. I can assure you they do not.

Let's get one thing straight before we go any further: These replicas are *not* U.S. government issues, no matter how official they may look—or how hard the clever advertisers work to blur the line. I decided to include them on my blacklist of "coin" losers not because they *are* coins, but rather because many potential buyers view them as a coin-related investment—and the advertisers foster that illusion. The language in the ads seems purposely designed to mislead unwary consumers into believing these offers are being made by an arm, or at least a close affiliate, of the federal government. The company will identify itself, for example, as "the National Mint" or "the Federal Mint"—names that suggest a link with Uncle Sam. There will be the ubiquitous certificate of authenticity—a guarantee essentially that the replicas contain the advertised amount of precious metal, which isn't really at issue. Most of all, the consumer will be overwhelmed and disarmed by that big, beautiful photograph showing what he or she knows to be a genuine (though now obsolete) U.S. coin design—only in a much larger reincarnation.

The bottom line is, these replicas are nothing more than supersized silver bars, worth only the value of the metal they contain, and yet they are priced much higher, as if they were coin collectibles. The only thing they will collect is dust; the only thing you will collect is red ink.

The 1943 "copper" cent

Few coins are as famous as the 1943 "copper" Lincoln cent, and few base-metal coins are more valuable. There is probably no other collectible coin that enjoys such wide appeal and instant recognition among the noncollecting American public. Truly, this is a rare coin for the masses.

For more than half a century, the '43 "copper penny" has been the subject of endless speculation, the stuff of urban legends, and the object of countless searches through cigar boxes, sugar bowls, and mayonnaise jars of old coins. All this attention has multiplied its value to collectors, which would have been considerable anyway, based on its genuine rarity. And largely *because* of this high profile, the coin is well worth the extra premium.

Like many coins of exceptional value, this one is imbued with history and romance. Its very existence resulted from a circumstance of history.

As 1942 drew to a close, World War II was at a critical juncture and certain resources—including copper—were urgently needed for combat-related purposes. To conserve this strategic metal, the U.S. Mint was directed to make cents in 1943 not from the normal bronze, an alloy with high copper content, but from zinc-coated steel, a composition that gave the coins a light gray appearance.

The experiment was abandoned in 1944, partly because of complaints that the cents looked confusingly like dimes. For the final two years of the war and one year thereafter, the Mint made cents from brass recovered from spent cartridge cases.

Rumors soon arose that a handful of 1943 cents had been struck in bronze by mistake—and for once the rumors turned out to be true. The first genuine example of such an error came to light in 1947, and since then a few others have surfaced—a total of about two dozen, from all three mints that made cents in 1943, but mostly from the main mint in Philadelphia. Their market value has risen steadily through the years, with several bringing six-figure sums. In *The Insider's Guide to U.S. Coin Values 2007*, I list the 1943-D bronze cent— the rarest and most valuable of the three—at $275,000 in Mint State-63 condition, the highest grade known. Even in the heavily circulated grade of Fine-12, the "S" and "P" varieties are listed at $60,000 and $42,000, respectively.

As you might expect, the high value of 1943 "coppers" has prompted many con artists to produce deceptive lookalikes, usually by copper-plating steel cents of that date. These are easy to detect because steel cents, unlike bronze cents, are attracted to a magnet. Some fast-buck operators tried a different tack, altering the final number on copper-alloy cents with similar dates, such as 1945 and 1948. Most of these alterations are obvious under a magnifying glass, but given the high value of genuine '43 bronze cents and the growing sophistication of some counterfeiters, it's essential to obtain third-party certification of any such coin.

Interestingly, most known examples of the 1943 "copper" cent show signs of wear and none is bright red, suggesting that these coins circulated fairly extensively before being found and set aside. This reinforces their appeal, for it underscores their mystique as what I call "pocket-change rarities"—valuable coins acquired at face value from circulation.

No further examples have been found in circulation for several decades, but hope springs eternal, and the search seems sure to go on from here to eternity. Even if no other example is ever found, the searching and the dreaming will keep this rare cent's image bright and ensure its permanent status as one of the most famous and desirable coins ever made by Uncle Sam—in short, a real winner.

LOSER

34 ⬇

Sets of 1946 through 1951 Booker T. Washington commemorative half dollars

By the late 1940s, commemorative coinage had fallen into disfavor with the U.S. government, and even with many collectors. Production of commemoratives had been on hold during World War II, but rather than being lifted after the end of the war, the suspension soon gave way to a virtual ban. Two commemoratives did win approval from Congress right after the war, one of which (the Booker T. Washington memorial half dollar) spawned a related coin honoring both Washington and a second black leader, George Washington Carver. But after the conclusion of the Washington-Carver program in 1954, no new U.S. commemoratives would appear for 28 years. The abuses surrounding such coins had left a sour taste in many people's mouths and built up a resistance to further issues.

The first postwar commemorative, the Iowa half dollar of 1946, was a one-year issue marking a statehood centennial—a theme that clearly merited such a coin. But the two subsequent coins, while laudable for honoring the achievements of black Americans, repeated some of the worst abuses linked to the many "commems" of the 1930s. The authorized mintage of 5 million Booker T. Washington halves (later shared with the Washington-Carver coin) was far too high. The programs were permitted to linger too long, extending all the way from1946 through 1954, with both types being produced in 1951. And serious questions arose as to whether the proceeds were benefiting worthy programs for blacks or simply lining the pockets of opportunistic sponsors.

Many Booker T. Washington halves went unsold and eventually were melted. More than 1.7 million survived, though—an enormously high number by the standards of "traditional" U.S. commemoratives. Further depressing their value, many were mishandled by the Mint itself, as the coins were not handled with care. Typically, these coins are sold in date-mint sets of P-D-S (Philadelphia, Denver, and San Francisco) issues. The 1946 through 1951 sets are the biggest losers among pre-1955 U.S. commemoratives, according to noted commemorative coin expert Anthony Swiatek. Their prices range from $110 to $150 in Mint State-63 or 64 (except for the 1949 set, which is valued at from $225 to $275), but they're ultra-common and all too often scuffed and unappealing.

Nickel three-cent pieces certified as Mint State-66 or 67

We've all heard it said that you shouldn't judge a book by its cover. For much the same reason, you shouldn't judge a coin by its mintage. Many coins that were made in meaningful quantities— even by the millions—are scarce or even rare in very high levels of preservation. Through wide circulation, mishandling, and other attrition, the mountain that existed at the time the coins were minted has shrunk to just a molehill in very high mint condition. The coins may be abundant in circulated grades and in lower mint-state levels and yet be downright rare in grades above Mint State-65—the so-called super-grade range.

Nickel three-cent pieces illustrate this point. These curious relics of the Reconstruction period after the Civil War were struck in significant numbers at the outset: Between their introduction in 1865 and 1870, more than 25 million pieces were produced. But those coins saw extensive use because they were sorely needed at a time when subsidiary silver coins (including the dime and half dime) hadn't yet begun to circulate widely after being hoarded during the war. Only a relative handful of nickel three-cent pieces from that early period ended up being preserved in pristine condition. Then, beginning in 1871, mintages dropped sharply as the new Shield nickel proved to be more popular with the public. Only proofs were issued in 1877 and 1878, and after one last burst of more than 1 million pieces in 1881, minuscule numbers of business strikes were issued through the end of the series in 1889.

Elsewhere in this book, I recommend nickel three-cent pieces in Proof-66 as one of my winners. Those are certainly rare and desirable, but these coins are even rarer in Mint State-66 and higher grades. The mintage figures belie that, as proofs exceeded 5,000 in only one year and fell below 1,000 in 10 other years. But many of those proofs were saved in top condition, and few of the business strikes were.

LOSER
35 ↓

The 1887/6 P-mint Morgan dollar graded Mint State-64 and higher

Overdates are among the most dramatic—and sometimes the most valuable—of mint-error U.S. coins. They were relatively common during the early years of the U.S. Mint, when budget constraints were severe, equipment was unsophisticated, and dies were often reused from one year to the next in an effort to hold down costs. They occurred far less frequently after the conversion to steam-powered coinage in the mid-1830s; the technological upgrade greatly enhanced the quality of the coins and quality control at the Mint. And they all but disappeared in the 20th century, so when overdates do appear, they bring exceptional premiums.

Typically, overdates have resulted when a die remained unused or only lightly used at the end of a calendar year and Mint technicians engraved a new last number over the old one so the die could continue to be used in the new year. On occasion, this process involved the last two numbers in the date—or even the last three, as when a die for 1798 was retooled for use in 1800. Because they occurred so frequently and were struck in such meaningful numbers, early U.S. overdates often command little or no more than regular coins from the same years. But modern U.S. overdates are quite a different story: The 1918/17-D Buffalo nickel, 1918/17-S Standing Liberty quarter, and 1942/1 Mercury dime all bring thousands of dollars in mint condition.

The 1887/6 Morgan dollar is far from common. But it also doesn't seem to be nearly as rare as the two 1918 overdates. And though it is part of a highly collected series, it never has attracted a fervent following. Undoubtedly this stems, in large measure, from the fact that the "6" isn't readily visible underneath the "7" in the date. It's so well concealed, in fact, that the overdate wasn't discovered until 1971. There are 1887/6 overdate dollars from both Philadelphia and New Orleans, with the O-mint coin being scarcer and more expensive. At $1,500 in MS-64 and $4,500 in MS-65, the P-mint overdate appears to be overpriced, since hundreds of examples have been certified in those grades. The supply exceeds the demand, and I would avoid this coin.

Lower-mintage American Eagle bullion coins, under certain circumstances

Not every "winner" comes without strings. Some are good values only to a point, or only under certain circumstances—and the number of strings attached may vary considerably from one item to another. I'm attaching several very important strings in recommending the purchase of American Eagle gold, silver, and platinum bullion coins.

American Eagles made their first appearance in 1986, when the U.S. Mint introduced the one-ounce silver Eagle plus gold Eagles in four versions: the basic one-ounce size and subsidiary sizes of ½, ¼, and ¹⁄₁₀ of an ounce. The platinum Eagle was added to the roster in 1997 and comes in the same four versions as its gold counterpart. As bullion coins, the business-strike American Eagles vary in price according to the value of the metal they contain; the price at any given time reflects their bullion value plus a small surcharge to cover the costs of production, distribution, and marketing. (This does not pertain to the proof American Eagles, which are listed as a "loser" elsewhere in this book.)

In theory, bullion coins are not numismatic in nature and bring no added premium as collectibles. In practice, some collectors do place added value on certain bullion coins when their mintages fall significantly below the normal production levels for their series. This premium may be modest, but it could have the potential to rise in years to come if a particular series continues to be produced and grows in popularity, thus expanding the circle of potential buyers for low-mintage dates. This brings me to the strings. I recommend these coins only if you pay no bonus premium to begin with (over the regular surcharge), and only if you buy them at a time when the price of bullion is not inflated. Half-ounce and quarter-ounce gold and platinum Eagles are especially good possibilities, since their mintages tend to be much lower than the one-ounce and tenth-ounce pieces. Michael R. Fuljenz of Universal Coins in Beaumont, Texas, says these coins offer what he calls a "double play" over ordinary bullion coins.

LOSER

36

Photograph courtesy the author

The Sacagawea dollar

The Sacagawea "golden dollar" coin has been one of the biggest disappointments in the U.S. Mint's history. Launched with high hopes and great fanfare in 2000, this artistically appealing "mini-dollar," which depicts a young Shoshone woman and her infant son, has been a dismal failure as a circulating coin. In fact, it hardly circulates at all. It hasn't done any better as a collectible. Made in huge quantities despite being shunned by the public, Sacagawea dollars hold little appeal for collectors and none at all for investors. And whatever aesthetic appeal they possess has a limited shelf life because these so-called golden dollars have a most unpleasant tendency to darken and turn drab with even limited use.

The term "golden dollar" is misleading: The Sacagawea dollar doesn't contain a speck of precious metal. It's made from a base-metal alloy of copper, zinc, manganese, and nickel, and while this combination produces a golden color when the coin is new, the chemically unstable manganese breaks down after even slight circulation, turning the surfaces dark and unattractive. Jefferson nickels made during World War II also contained manganese and also became unsightly with use, so the Mint should have known it might happen this time, too.

This image problem is more than skin-deep, though. By calling the coins "golden dollars" in a nationwide publicity campaign, the Mint created the widespread illusion that they *did* contain gold, which led many uninformed Americans to set the coins aside when they first appeared, rather than spending them. As a result, gaining acceptance for the Sacagawea as a circulating coin became an even more daunting task for the government. In 2002, after having made more than 1.4 billion Sacagawea dollars for use in commerce, the Mint threw in the towel on further mass production. Since then, it has made much smaller numbers—roughly between 5 million and 8 million a year—strictly for sale to collectors at a premium.

As mentioned previously in this book, most of the base-metal dollar coins issued by the U.S. Mint during the past few decades have been big losers. Business-strike Eisenhower dollars in very high grades are exceptions to this rule, at least in the eyes of collectors, because they are so scarce in choice condition. But Susan B. Anthony dollars are losers on everyone's list and Sacagawea dollars are failures, too, for pretty much the same reasons. The public doesn't use them, collectors don't collect them, and investors don't invest in them. In baseball terms, I'd call that "Strike one, strike two, strike three!"

The lower-mintage dollars made since 2002 have somewhat greater potential. But 5 million isn't a low mintage in absolute terms. And the Mint took a bite out of any future gain by selling the coins at a premium at the outset. Beyond that, the coins' metallic instability makes it harder to preserve them in pristine mint condition and riskier to pay bonus prices for higher-grade specimens.

Warning: Sacagawea dollars are scheduled to be made in large quantities again starting in 2007. In authorizing a series of circulating $1 coins to honor the nation's presidents, Congress has ordered resumption of production of the Sacagaweas as well. Both kinds will be "golden dollars." And both, I am quite certain, will be losers.

These coins are available in all grades in tremendous quantities. Beware of Proof- and Mint State-69 and 70 examples offered with large price tags on television shopping networks.

The 1861-O Liberty Head double eagle graded AU-50

With the outbreak of the Civil War on April 12, 1861, three of the four branch mints then in operation were behind Confederate lines. Only the main mint in Philadelphia and the branch in San Francisco remained in Union hands. The War Between the States was the death knell for the mints in Charlotte, North Carolina, and Dahlonega, Georgia, but the third Southern mint—in New Orleans—resumed its role as a federal institution in the late 1870s, first as an assay office in 1876 and then as a mint in 1879. It continued producing coins until 1909.

Limited numbers of U.S. coins were struck at New Orleans in 1861, before and after the mint fell into Confederate hands. It actually functioned as a federal agency for only a month that year: The state of Louisiana took charge of all operations on January 31, 1861, and the Confederate States of America then assumed control on March 31. Old records show that the Confederate forces found more than $200,000 worth of bullion in the vaults and struck this into coinage—using U.S. dies—before closing the mint on May 31 because it had no further metal to coin.

Half dollars and double eagles ($20 gold pieces) were the only coins produced in New Orleans in that fateful first year of the war. The half dollar mintage was relatively high, totaling more than 2.5 million—and even though most of these were struck under state or Confederate auspices, all were made with U.S. dies, so there's no way of telling them apart. (It's believed that four half dollars bearing a Confederate reverse also were minted in 1861 in New Orleans.) By contrast, the O mint produced just 17,741 double eagles—presumably because it ran out of bullion at that point. These are virtually unknown in mint condition and the few known examples bring exceptional premiums. Even then, you're apt to find wear on the high points. Nice examples graded About Uncirculated-50 can be had for $23,000 or so, and I recommend these. They're rare coins from a pivotal year in U.S. and U.S. Mint history.

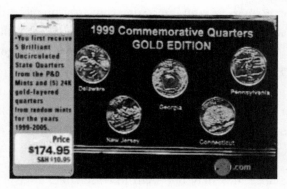

Gold and platinum "layered" coins

Home-shopping TV shows have found many ways to foist fifth-rate coins on unsuspecting customers under the guise of being first-rate bargains. It would be hard to find a more flagrant example of misleading marketing, however, than the "gold-layered" and "platinum-layered" coins breathlessly touted by shameless shills as truly exceptional buys.

The TV hucksters start with coins of low value but high popular appeal. Among their favorites are the circulating commemorative coins issued by the U.S. Mint in its 50 State Quarters Program. Since 1999, the Mint has been producing special Washington quarters, at the rate of five per year, honoring the 50 states of the Union. These coins have caught Americans' fancy, and millions of people have been setting them aside, seeking to assemble sets of all 50—perhaps one of each from both mints (Philadelphia and Denver) making them for use in circulation. This may take time, but it isn't an insuperable task, since the Mint produces hundreds of millions of each state quarter at each of the two locations. State quarters are readily available from reputable coin dealers for modest premiums, even in mint condition.

A set of state quarters is an interesting conversation piece, but by no means is it scarce and valuable. That doesn't stop the TV shills from saying it is, however. But then the home-shopping shows go one step further: They get the coins "layered" with a micron-thin plating of gold or platinum, put them in fancy packages, and charge even fancier prices—sometimes $15 per coin, or hundreds of dollars for a complete set of all 50 quarters from both mints (with later coins to be shipped and paid for as they are issued).

At first glance, this may not seem unreasonable; after all, gold is worth hundreds of dollars an ounce. The TV pitchmen certainly make it sound like a golden opportunity. The truth of the matter is that there's precious little gold and absolutely no opportunity—except to lose money. The syndicated TV program *Inside Edition* had a group of these coins analyzed in the spring of 2006, and its experts made some startling discoveries. At a time when gold was selling for more than $700 an ounce, the gold "layered" to each statehood quarter was worth less than two cents. Worse yet, when two independent testing laboratories examined five-cent coins supposedly layered with platinum, *Inside Edition* reported that they "couldn't find any platinum at all."

Ironically, the layering (if any) detracts from the coins' value as collectibles, rather than enhancing it. True collectors look askance at such tinkering, viewing it almost as they would a scratch or gouge—as a form of defacement. This attitude applies to any such modification done outside the mint where the coins were made, whether the added element is gold, platinum, patriotic colors, or a picture of Elvis Presley. Far from making them more desirable, the process destroys any premium value the coins may have had on their own. Quite literally, it's a case of subtraction by addition.

I assisted *Inside Edition* in its painstaking investigation of this and other abuses by home-shopping TV coin shows and appeared in its televised report, which aired in mid-May of 2006. Despite my familiarity with the overall problem, even I was taken aback by the metallurgical findings and the almost total worthlessness of the layered (or, in some cases, *allegedly* layered) coins.

One final piece of advice: When using your TV remote control to channel-surf, avoid the home-shopping coin shows. Watch *Inside Edition* instead.

The 1885-CC Morgan dollar graded Mint State-65

In recent years, the term *condition rarity* has become an important part of the coin market's lexicon. This phrase describes a coin that may be rather common—with a modest price to match—in lower grade levels, but is scarce or flat-out rare and brings a first-rate premium in pristine mint condition. The Morgan dollar series includes a number of coins that fit this description. Consider, for example, the 1886-O. This coin can be purchased for $10 or less in Very Fine—a mid-level circulated grade—but its price soars into the thousands in Mint State-63, into the tens of thousands in Mint State-65, and into the hundreds of thousands in Mint State-66.

Accurate grading is crucial when just a small difference in grade can translate into a difference of many thousands of dollars in market value. Likewise, it is essential to preserve such a coin with extraordinary care and protect it from the slightest imperfection. Even then, there is a risk that the price of a mint-state specimen could be affected adversely—and possibly plunge precipitously—if hitherto unknown supplies of the coin turn up in top condition. After all, the New Orleans Mint made 10.7 million dollars in 1886.

No such worries exist with a silver dollar struck just one year earlier at the Carson City Mint. The 1885-CC Morgan dollar is rare in *every* condition because the Nevada mint produced just 228,000 cart-wheels that year—the fourth-lowest mintage in the Morgan series. A circulated piece will cost you much more than the corresponding 1886-O; even in the grade of Extremely Fine, for instance, the '85-CC dollar sells for nearly $600. But there are no huge increments as you go up the grading scale. On the contrary, the jumps are quite small until you reach the high mint-state range. This rare-date coin can be obtained for less than $1,300 in MS-65 and less than $2,600 in MS-66. True, this reflects the fact that much of the mintage survives in uncirculated condition, having been stored for decades in U.S. Treasury vaults. But given the low mintage, the current market val-ues have a bedrock base of rarity. And you can go to bed not having to worry that your rare, beautiful coin—struck at a colorful mint spawned by the historic Comstock Lode—will lose much of its value overnight.

Carson City dollars in U.S. government General Services Adminis-tration (G.S.A.) sealed cases are often worthy of a premium, espe-cially if NGC has offered its opinion as to the coin's grade and affixed its hologram to the holder. Coins in these holders, sold by the G.S.A. to the public from 1972 to 1980, can be considered original and not tampered with. This is an excellent safeguard for collectors concerned about coins being doctored or altered after they leave the mint. But be careful not to get too enthusiastic over the concept of a sealed government holder and an NGC grade: Sometimes these coins will sell for hundreds of dollars more just because they are in G.S.A. holders. Crack the holder, and you will never be able to re-cover the premium.

LOSER

38 ⬇ Legal-tender coins produced by private mints such as The Franklin Mint for issuance by foreign governments

There is a long tradition in the United States of private companies striking fine-art medals. The earliest presidential inaugural badges and medals, for example, were produced by such firms as Whitehead and Hoag of Newark, New Jersey, and the Joseph K. Davison Company of Philadelphia. Later, Medallic Art Company of New York City played a key role in designing and producing inaugural medals, as well as other medals, such as the twice-yearly Society of Medalists issues.

None of this adequately prepared the numismatic community for the whirlwind arrival of a new kind of private minter in the mid-1960s. Founded in 1965 as General Numismatics Corp., the company soon transformed itself into a marketing giant known as The Franklin Mint. Instead of producing and selling art medals one at a time, this new "mint" launched whole series of glitzy silver medals built around such themes as "The History of the United States" and "The Genius of Michelangelo." A typical series consisted of perhaps 60 one-ounce silver proof medals that would be shipped one a month until the collection was completed. Orders would be "limited"—but only to the number submitted by a given deadline (only one subscription per customer, please).

The Franklin Mint spawned numerous imitators, and for a time the marketplace was deluged not only with private medals but also with such related items as ingots, bars, plates, and even spoons. Eventually, the craze subsided and the companies either diversified or withered on the vine. Some, including The Franklin Mint, used their production capacity to strike increasing numbers of legal-tender coins for foreign governments. But the customers tended to be small nations seeking big revenue from selling "collectible" coins at inflated prices. Some of these coins are gold platinum; others come in sets or whole series. Either way, they can cost many hundreds of dollars. They're not worth it, and you should avoid them like the plague they are.

WINNER 39

Type 2 and 3 Liberty Head double eagles graded Mint State-60 through 63

The Saint-Gaudens double eagle is the superstar of U.S. gold coinage, and the elegant, full-length Liberty depicted on its obverse is the glamorous leading lady who always gets rave reviews from the critics. The Liberty Head that adorns all previous double eagles seems matronly and sedate—perhaps a character actress—by comparison. Looks can be deceiving, though. While those earlier coins are clearly not as glitzy as and lack the marquee value of the aptly nicknamed "Saints," they're often more solid performers at the box office for their backers—the collectors and investors who rely on them as a source of financial gain. Put another way, Liberty Head double eagles—particularly the later ones—are generally scarcer and more valuable than the glamour-puss coins that succeeded them.

The double eagle, or $20 gold piece, came into being in 1849 as a direct result of the California Gold Rush. Needing new ways to utilize all the gold that was pouring into the marketplace, Congress authorized two new gold coins—this nearly one-ounce heavyweight and the tiny gold dollar—to help soak up the excess supply. The basic design of the Liberty double eagle remained much the same throughout its more than 50-year run, but collectors recognize three distinct types. The original version gave way to Type 2 in 1866, when the motto IN GOD WE TRUST was added to the reverse. Then, in 1877, Type 3 came about when the statement of value was changed from the shorthand TWENTY D. to TWENTY DOLLARS.

Michael R. Fuljenz of Universal Coin and Bullion in Beaumont, Texas, reports that Type 2 and 3 examples of this coin in mint condition are "much rarer" than Saints in mint condition—presumably because they weren't set aside to nearly the same extent when they were new. Original bags of Saints turn up much more frequently, and in much larger quantities, than bags of Mint State Liberties, Fuljenz says. And when gold bullion goes up in value, late-date "Libs" tend to rise the fastest.

This coin is listed as a winner, as I am optimistic about the outlook for gold. However, if you see gold bullion decreasing in value dramatically, you can reasonably expect Type 2 and 3 Liberty Head double eagles graded Mint State-60 through 63 to be big losers if you purchased them when gold was higher. Further, Section 352 of the U.S. Patriot Act could significantly affect the investment attractiveness of these "Libs," as many dealers of these kinds of gold coins are now required to keep detailed records of transactions to comply with anti–money laundering requirements that are now being enforced.

In October 2006, with gold at $600 per ounce, a common date Type 3 Liberty Head double eagle retails for $700 in MS-60, $725 in MS-61, $750 in MS-62, and $850 in MS-63. Type 2 is rarer and, thus, more expensive.

Fractional gold pieces graded Mint State-63 through 65

LOSER
39 ⬇

Good things come in small packages, or so we are told. In practice, of course, this is true only part of the time. Even when good things do come in small packages, they may be good only to a point, or only under certain circumstances. If that point is exceeded, or those circumstances cease to exist, the contents of those "packages" may not be so good after all. Consider the case of the fractional gold coins minted in California during and after the famous Gold Rush.

California was awash in gold dust and nuggets in the early 1850s as prospectors worked their claims and brought their ore to market. What it lacked most conspicuously was a standard and convenient medium of exchange—in short, small coinage—since gold in raw form left much to be desired in this regard. To fill this pressing need, private minters began producing small gold coin substitutes for U.S. coins valued at $1 and under in 1852, assigning denominations of dollar, half dollar, and quarter dollar. These supplemented the higher-value gold pieces, in denominations of $5 through $50, which also were being privately struck at that time. The small-denomination gold assumed a lesser role following the opening of the San Francisco Mint in 1854, which soon provided the region with official U.S. coinage of comparable face value. They remained popular, though, as souvenirs and continued to be minted until 1882.

Thousands of these small gold pieces survive today, in hundreds of varieties. Many are quite rare, and all command at least modest premiums. Typically, they are worth about $600 each in mid-range mint condition—the range represented by MS-63 through 65. Pricing them is difficult, however, because they are so rare and esoteric. And, for this reason, unscrupulous telemarketers love to sell them, frequently charging up to 20 times their actual market value. Thus, while these small "packages" are surely rare and valuable—in other words, *good*—they are overpriced so often that it would be advisable to avoid them as if they were really *bad*.

An 1877-S Liberty Head double eagle graded Mint State-62

At first glance, the 1877-S Liberty Head double eagle (or $20 gold piece) seems to be a coin of no particular interest, with a relatively high mintage by the standards of its series and denomination. Indeed, at 1,735,000, it has the second-highest mintage of any "Lib $20" struck between 1862 and 1897—just 4,000 pieces behind the pacesetter, the 1878-S. On closer inspection, however, this turns out to be a rare coin in pristine mint condition—in fact, in any grade above the modest level of Mint State-62.

There are various reasons why a coin produced in large numbers may be surprisingly scarce in high grades. One of the most common explanations is that the coin had generally poor quality to begin with so that few, if any, examples existed in flawless condition even on the day they left the mint. That's a major reason so many of our modern copper-nickel "clad" coins are elusive in the upper-end mint state grades. Mishandling is another contributing factor, and this appears to have been a serious problem with Lib-

SCOTT TRAVERS' TOP 88 COINS TO BUY & SELL

erty Head double eagles. The late Walter Breen, perhaps the most renowned of all numismatic researchers, reported in his *Complete Encyclopedia of U.S. and Colonial Coins* that many of these large gold coins "occur without discernible wear but with some hair and feather details obscured by bag marks." He went on to say that these coins usually are regarded—and priced—as AU, rather than uncirculated.

Whatever the reason, experience has shown that the 1877-S double eagle is rare in even mid-level mint state grades—and this is reflected in its price: It brings more than $15,000 in MS-63. By contrast, it is readily available in grades below that level, selling for a much more affordable $3,000 in MS-62, just a single grade down the ladder. As you might expect, that makes it quite easy to sell this coin when it is certified as MS-62. The chances of getting it regraded as MS-63 are remote, since the grading services are keenly aware of the price gap and reluctant to create instant wealth.

LOSER

40

Photograph courtesy U.S. Mint

The American Buffalo bullion gold coin certified as Mint State or Proof-70 First Strike

For nearly a century, the Buffalo nickel has been one of Americans' favorite coins. Its evocative design, portraying a Native American chief on the obverse and an American bison on the reverse, calls to mind immediately the rugged, romantic days of the nation's Old West, one of the most colorful and dramatic periods in American history.

It's little wonder, then, that coin collectors have lavished huge amounts of attention, affection, and money on the original Buffalo nickel series, which was struck for circulation from 1913 to 1938. Nor is it surprising that the series has performed exceptionally well through the years, rewarding careful buyers with significant returns on their investments.

The U.S. Mint is keenly aware of the Buffalo nickel's broad appeal to collectors and deep admiration by the general public. As a result, it has used very similar designs on several commemorative and bullion coins in recent years, hoping this appeal would help boost demand for these coins, increasing sales and revenues. A case in point was the American Bison commemorative silver dollar issued in 2001 to raise funds for the National Museum of the American Indian. This coin—virtually identical in design to the Buffalo nickel—had a modest mintage limit of 500,000 and sold out in just two weeks, largely because of the design.

In mid-2006, the Mint introduced a one-ounce gold bullion coin with a fineness of 0.9999—the purest gold coin in U.S. history. And again, it turned to the Buffalo nickel, using that coin's design almost exactly as it appeared in its original form. The combination of 24-karat gold and magnificent artwork electrified the marketplace, creating enormous demand for this undeniably dazzling new coin. Within days, it was making enormous inroads into the market shares of long-established gold bullion coins of similar high purity, notably Canada's Maple Leaf.

Given all this, many might assume it's a foregone conclusion that I would enthusiastically list the American Buffalo Gold Coin, as it's called by the Mint, as a big winner. And if it is purchased solely as a bullion coin, worth just the value of the gold (about $600 per ounce as this is written) it contains plus a nominal premium, there's every reason to think that it does have a bright future. Unfortunately, the coin's tremendous popularity has given rise to high-priced versions that can only be described as horrible buys. They are, in fact, the absolute worst buys in the entire coin market as of this writing in October 2006.

The versions to be avoided at all costs—and their costs have been astoundingly high—are uncirculated American Buffaloes graded Mint State-70 and proofs graded Proof-70 DCAM (Deep Cameo) "First Strike" by certification services such as the Professional Coin

Grading Service (PCGS) and the Numismatic Guaranty Corporation of America (NGC). These coins have been trading for $3,000 apiece and more—often much more.

People buying such coins, and paying such outrageous premiums, are applying standards meant for high-grade business strikes of coins whose series saw extensive circulation. Relatively few coins in those series survive in top condition, so the few remaining "gems" command—and are worth—big money. Bullion coins, by contrast, do not circulate, so high-grade examples are the rule and not the exception. Paying thousands of dollars for one of these coins simply because it's better than average in appearance is, quite frankly, a terrible waste of money. And I can see no way that such a misguided "investment" will ever be recouped.

The U.S. Mint has even weighed in on the subject. Perhaps to nip in the bud what it views as an abuse of the new bullion program, the Mint issued a statement in the late summer of 2006 seeking to discredit the use of the term *first strike* by sellers marketing high-priced American Buffaloes.

"Currently," it said, "there is no widely accepted and standardized numismatic industry definition of 'first strike.' Coin dealers and grading services may use this term in varying ways."

It went on to say: "The United States Mint has not designated any 2005 or 2006 American Eagle Coins or 2006 American Buffalo Coins as 'first strikes,' nor do we track the order in which we mint such coins during their production."

I do not always see eye-to-eye with the U.S. Mint's policies and practices, and quite a few of the "losers" in this book landed in that category because of poor decisions by the Mint. In this case, though, the

Mint has served a useful purpose by planting seeds of doubt about extravagantly overpriced coins. Moreover, its statement—certain to dampen sales of these coins—provides yet another reason for avoiding them.

American Buffaloes are majestic in appearance and desirable as stores of precious metal. But stripped of the glitter and hype, they're bullion coins and not numismatic treasures. And that's how buyers should treat them.

WINNER 41

The 1849 Liberty double eagle

Double eagles ($20 gold pieces) were the highest-denomination coins ever struck for circulation by Uncle Sam, and they had the highest intrinsic value, because each contained just under an ounce of gold. Those qualities alone give these coins special appeal to collectors and noncollectors alike. By an odd twist of fate, however, the very first and very last double eagles are the two most valuable. Both, in fact, rank among the greatest rarities in all of U.S. numismatics.

The last double eagle, dated 1933, has been much in the news lately. This coin, designed by famed sculptor Augustus Saint-Gaudens, was treated for decades as contraband subject to seizure by the federal government (see **LOSER 1**). Then, in 2002, when federal officials permitted the sale of one—and only one—specimen, it brought $7.59 million, the highest price ever paid for a single U.S. coin at a public sale. In 2005, 10 more examples came to light and were confiscated by the government. Their ultimate fate remains in doubt.

The first double eagle, dated 1849, is even rarer—and, if sold, undoubtedly would bring much more than $7.59 million. In fact, I estimate its value at $12 million in *The Insider's Guide to U.S. Coin Values 2007*. The key words are "if sold," for only two examples reportedly were struck, and just one can be accounted for today. That one is in the National Numismatic Collection at the Smithsonian Institution and therefore unlikely to be offered for sale. By contrast, 445,500 examples of the 1933 Saint-Gaudens double eagle were produced, and though almost all were melted and only one is legal to own today, the potential exists for many more to appear on the market someday. As it is, at least 11 are known to exist even now.

The 1849 double eagle is a true '49-er—a direct result of the California Gold Rush. Its introduction coincided with the arrival of thousands of fortune-hunters in California following the discovery of gold at Sutter's Mill in 1848. Congress authorized this coin, along with the gold dollar, to provide a convenient means to store the yellow metal in a form that was easy to spend.

Although the new coins were authorized in February 1849, production of double eagles didn't start until 1850. They bore a design by the Mint's chief sculptor-engraver, James B. Longacre, showing Liberty wearing a coronet—a portrait very much like the one already in use for a decade or more on smaller gold coins.

Mint records state that two trial strikes, both proofs, were made on March 12, 1850, before the start of regular production for that year, and both were dated 1849. One was the coin now in the national collection. The other reportedly was presented to William M. Meredith, then the secretary of the Treasury, and later sold as part of his estate. Its location has been unknown for many years.

Collectors have long considered the 1849 double eagle an unattainable rarity, a view reinforced by the fact that it has never appeared in a public sale. But it's not far-fetched to think that one of the two specimens—possibly even both—might become available to buyers with very deep pockets in the not-too-distant future. Owners have a way of locating "missing" rarities when similar coins bring exceptional prices, as happened in 2003 when a million-dollar offer led to the rediscovery of a 1913 Liberty Head nickel hidden in a closet for more than 40 years.

If and when an 1849 double eagle does come up for sale, it will almost certainly zoom to the top of the list as the highest-priced coin in history. And it will be worth every cent. This is more than a great rarity—it's a transcendently rare coin spawned by one of the epochal events in U.S. history and a coin that marked the birth of one of the most highly coveted series in the annals of American numismatics.

Average high-grade coins from buried treasure, shipwrecks, and hoards when first brought to market

Buried treasure has always held great allure for men of adventure and action. The thought of discovering old oaken chests full of hidden pirate booty, or sunken Spanish galleons at the bottom of the sea with cargos of glittering gold, can fire the imagination like few other visions known to man. Ironically, however, the appearance of such treasure in centuries-old graves can jeopardize the value of wealth already secured in safes and under mattresses. Likewise, coins held in hoards for many years can depress market values for similar coins already in collections.

Gold is impervious, or at least highly resistant, to damage from natural forces such as water coursing through a sunken ship. As a consequence, golden treasure recovered from salvaged ships often will betray little evidence of the elements to which it has been subjected. Gold coins, in particular, have emerged from such vessels in remarkably high levels of preservation. And, in recent years, as technology has improved and the heightened price of gold has justified greater outlays by investors, salvagers have grown more and more aggressive in exploring shipwreck sites—and more and more successful in finding and recovering long-lost treasure.

The 1854-S double eagle, the very first $20 gold piece struck at the fledgling San Francisco Mint, has turned up in meaningful quantities in the bowels of several salvaged 19th-century ships, including the SS *Yankee Blade* and the SS *Central America*. Discoveries such as these can destabilize and reduce the value of scarce-date gold coins as collectibles. This has happened already with the 1854-S double eagle, a better-date coin worth thousands of dollars in mint condition. And it can happen again as new treasure is salvaged and hits the market. Similarly, the market absorbed 15,000 high-grade examples of the 1908 no-motto Saint-Gaudens double eagle that came from the so-called Wells-Fargo Hoard. Until the process of absorption is complete, this overhang is bound to hold prices down.

Treasure coins are often marketed with much hoopla and glitz and sold for prices that justify the marketing programs. After the excitement fades, so do the high prices. Treasure coins are winners if you buy them after they have been brought to market at significant discounts from their original offering prices. The winners in treasure coins are the marketers—and the one or two well-connected collectors who buy the highest-graded coin or two out of the tens of thousands of specimens curated and certified.

WINNER
42 ▲ The 1875 Liberty Head eagle graded About Uncirculated-50

When is a "rare coin" really, truly rare? The answer isn't always as obvious as you might think. The 1877 Indian cent, for example, certainly is perceived as being rare and would hold a high place on most collectors' wish lists, yet it has a mintage of 852,500. There are only two half cents with mintages higher than that, yet half cents as a group are looked upon by most as scarce, rather than rare. Likewise, the 1916-D Mercury dime is viewed by just about everyone as a rare coin, but its mintage of 264,000 is higher than that of the 1869 Seated Liberty dime (256,000), which is considered a fairly common coin within its series.

In both of these illustrations, rarity is relative. Indian cents are collected far more widely than half cents, so a coin can be deemed a rarity even with a mintage that would be quite high in a different series. Similarly, there are many more collectors pursuing sets of Mercury dimes than sets of Seated dimes, so the standards are different. Intensify the demand in the law of supply and demand and you increase the value of any given coin; value, in turn, reinforces the perception of rarity.

There are some cases, of course, where rarity is absolute—where mintages are so minuscule that everyone agrees the coins on a given list are flat-out rare. The 1875 Liberty Head eagle is such a coin. Only 100 business strikes and 20 proofs were made that year at the Philadelphia Mint, making this the lowest-mintage $10 gold piece in U.S. history. As if that didn't make it rare enough, many examples are thought to have been melted soon after being struck. Production of gold coins was at low ebb in the mid-1870s, largely because of reduced demand from banks, which were balking at redeeming paper money, including federal notes, with gold and silver coins. The 1875 eagle is all but unknown in mint condition, making AU-50 the highest collectible grade. It's priced at $90,000, but other eagles from the same period with mintages in the thousands don't bring a whole lot less, so in reality this is a wonderful buy.

LOSER
42 ⬇

The 1914 Indian Head quarter eagle graded Mint State-62

Price guides are excellent tools for people who buy and sell coins. Few people—even experts—can memorize the value of every single coin, in every single grade, with unfailing accuracy, so price guides play a vital role in filling in buyers' and sellers' mental blanks. But even the finest price guides aren't perfect, and no price guide, however venerable and respected it may be, should ever be regarded as infallible.

In a fluid marketplace such as the one for coins, prices can change quickly and dramatically, so many of the prices in popular guidebooks, and even in weekly periodicals, are bound to be at variance with actual market values at any given time. I recognize this in preparing my own annual price guide, *The Insider's Guide to U.S. Coin Values*. I strive to make each price as accurate as possible on the date it is submitted to the publisher, taking into account any major trends I perceive, either upward or downward. But I realize that this book, and other listings like it, are, after all, simply *guides*, as their names suggest.

Outright mistakes are another matter. Now and then, a price guide or several price guides will list a coin's value far higher or lower than what that coin is bringing in the marketplace. Occasionally, such an error persists in future listings, rather like a lie that assumes the appearance of truth through repeated restatements. A coin such as this has fallen through the cracks, so to speak. An excellent example is the 1914 Indian Head quarter eagle certified in the grade of Mint State-62. This coin is wrongly perceived to be scarcer and more valuable than it really is. Perhaps this is because at 240,117, it has the lowest mintage of any Philadelphia issue in its series and the second-lowest overall, behind the genuinely scarce 1911-D (at 55,680). But it is only marginally scarcer than the so-called common coins in the series priced at the $500 level. And at $3,000, its price in some listings is double or more what it sells for among knowledgeable dealers and collectors. Pay that kind of money and you might see your potential profit fall between the cracks as well.

Early $2½, $5, and $10 gold pieces in mint condition

Early U.S. gold coins are wonderful buys in any collectible grade and are extremely attractive, both aesthetically and as investments, in EF and AU condition, as I noted in naming them **WINNER 28.** However, they are in a class by themselves in mint condition. In fact, early gold pieces graded MS-63, 64, and 65 are the most important coins in the marketplace as this is written in October 2006. And they will remain so as long as gold continues to increase in value.

Like their circulated counterparts, mint state early gold coins are truly rare, have a solid collector base, hold great appeal for investors, and enjoy an outstanding track record in the marketplace. What sets them apart from the rest is their dazzling appearance. Early gold coins graded EF and AU are beautiful, but in MS-63, 64, and 65, they're magnificent—miniature works of art that would look right at home in a gallery or museum.

In 1979 and 1980, when gold bullion soared to an all-time record high of more than $875 an ounce internationally, the entire coin market experienced a boom. The impact was enormous across the board. When gold began surging again a quarter-century later, early gold coins got a much bigger boost than anything else. Already strong, the coin market drew further energy from the bullion-buying binge. But this time, the flame was far more intense and much more sharply focused under one specific area: early gold coins in mint condition.

As this is written, these coins are on fire. Everyone who can afford them wants to buy them, and collectors, investors, and even dealers are throwing away their price guides when they bid on them at auctions. It's not unusual to see such a coin with a price-guide value of $40,000 bring $90,000 or more at an auction. This is a textbook case of supply and demand: Very few of these coins are available, and the universe wants to buy them. With early gold coins, the momentum has been fueled by gold's continuing surge and the powerful demand from determined buyers. And both of these propellants seem likely to persist. Under such circumstances, that $90,000 early gold coin—far from being overpriced—may look like a bargain before long.

As long as gold continues to rise in value, mint state early gold coins will be at the top of my list of winners to buy and hold. These are the coins you should be pursuing if you want to maximize your gold-related gains in the current marketplace.

LOSER
43

The 1936 Cleveland commemorative half dollar graded Mint State-65

Cleveland is a city with much to offer. In recent years, it has become the home of the Rock and Roll Hall of Fame and a beautiful new stadium, Jacobs Field. The stadium, in turn, has brought even brighter luster to the city and its people through the on-the-field success of baseball's Cleveland Indians, who play their home games at that facility. Despite these upbeat developments, though, Cleveland continues to suffer lingering image problems because of bad publicity in the past.

Perhaps those image problems have rubbed off on the Cleveland half dollar, the special 50-cent piece struck by the U.S. Mint in 1936 to commemorate the centennial of the city on Lake Erie's southern shore. The centennial gave rise to a celebration called the Great Lakes Exposition, which took place in Cleveland in 1936, and the coin was sold to visitors for $1.50 each to raise needed revenue to help finance that event. It's worth a good deal more than that today, but not nearly as much as some of the other commemorative coins from the same period. And, like the city it honors, it doesn't always get a lot of respect.

Congress authorized a minimum of 25,000 Cleveland half dollars and a maximum of 50,000. The Mint struck 25,000 initially; then, when those sold out, it produced the entire remaining authorization. An overhang was left when the exposition closed, but the sponsors chose not to return any unsold coins for melting, diverging in that regard from a practice that was followed with numerous other commemoratives. As a result, supplies of this coin have always been more than adequate to satisfy collector demand and prices have been modest: Even in Mint State-65, it retails as of this writing for only about $300. All of this makes the coin accessible and affordable. But since there is strong supply and limited demand, it also makes for a coin with little investment potential. In short, this is one instance in which lack of respect appears to be fully justified.

1798-1807 Capped Bust quarter eagles graded Extremely Fine-45

Two dollars and 50 cents won't go very far today. It's hardly enough to rent a video, much less cover the price of admission to see a first-run movie in a theater. It may be enough for a Kid's Meal at McDonald's, but it won't buy mom or dad a Big Mac. This now-puny sum was far from inconsequential, though, in America's formative years. At the start of the 19th century, $2.50 would have bought a bushel of salt, a substance essential to keep meat from spoiling in that era without refrigeration. For many working people, in fact, it represented a full week's wages at the time.

It's little wonder, then, that the quarter eagle (or $2.50 gold piece) was struck in such small numbers in the period when U.S. coinage, like the nation itself, was very young. From 1796, when the coin made its first appearance, through 1807, when the initial design type—the Capped Bust Facing Right—ran its course, the quarter eagle was issued in eight years, yet the total combined mintage for that entire period was less than 20,000. That kind of figure is looked upon as rare when it constitutes the mintage for a year, much less a series.

More than one-third of the Capped Bust Facing Right quarter eagles were struck in 1807, the last year before the design was changed. In fact, that year's mintage of 6,812 was more than twice the combined output of the second- and third-place years, 1804 and 1802, respectively. The greater availability of the coins struck from 1798 through 1807 has enhanced their popularity as type coins, since some of the 1796 and 1797 dates are prohibitively rare, with price tags to match. Even the 1807 is all but unobtainable in uncirculated condition; it costs $32,500 in the lowest mint state grade, MS-60. But it's far more available, and affordable, in EF-45, a grade in which it's now priced at $12,000. And a true EF specimen retains a substantial amount of mint luster. Given the rarity of *any* coin from this series, that's not much to pay for a piece that's bright, appealing, and close to new.

1924-S, 1925-S, and 1928-S Peace dollars graded Mint State-65

The Peace dollar is widely considered to be one of the most attractive coins ever issued by Uncle Sam. This is due primarily to its compelling portraiture—fresh, modern depictions of Miss Liberty on the obverse and an eagle at rest on the reverse. But it's also due to the unusual openness of the design, free from the clutter and elaborate detail that make many other coins seem too "busy."

Unfortunately, the short life span of this much-admired dollar, from 1921 to 1935, fell largely within a period when U.S. coins in general weren't sharply struck. The Peace dollar was no exception, and the preponderance of "weak strikes" combined with the paucity of detail in the design have made this series a real challenge for coin-grading services. On the one hand, the broad, open design magnifies imperfections, making well-struck, high-grade examples extremely scarce. At the same time, the absence of intricate detail deprives graders of diagnostic elements that make other coins (the Morgan dollar, for instance) relatively easy to grade. Without such points of reference, graders find it much more difficult to differentiate, say, a Mint State-65 specimen from an MS-64.

The grading problem, in turn, has magnified a serious pricing problem. Because they are so scarce in grades of MS-65 and above, Peace dollars command big premiums in those grades—often thousands of dollars. Their market value drops significantly, though, in grades below MS-65 because such coins are much more plentiful. And that's the rub: A coin in a holder that reads MS-65—and priced at $15,000—may actually be a high-end MS-64 example that should be worth only $1,250. And this kind of slight (but costly) overgrading occurs all too often because of the unusual difficulty involved in accurate grading of this series.

During the 1920s, weak strikes were particularly common at the branch mint in San Francisco, where extended use of worn dies seems to have exacerbated the already significant problem. Three Peace dollars from that decade—the 1924-S, 1925-S, and 1928-S—cause the most trouble: Not only are they scuffed and chronically lacking in sharp detail, but their market value soars in the one-point increment from MS-64 to 65.

"There are no clear-cut criteria as to whether these coins are 64's or 65's," California coin dealer Steve Contursi complains. "These coins, especially the 1928-S in MS-65, represent a very dangerous area in the market."

Contursi accuses the grading services of "consciously controlling the MS-65 output of these dates" as a result of graders realizing that this coin in MS-65 is worth thousands of dollars more than its counterpart in MS-64.

There's a two-pronged risk in buying MS-65 Peace dollars at the prices being charged as this is written, in October 2006. If the two leading grading services, PCGS and NGC, modify their standards in an effort to address the uncertainties and inaccuracies now besetting the series, they may upgrade many of the coins currently graded MS-64, substantially increasing the number of MS-65 examples and reducing the value of your $15,000 coin to $7,500 or less. Worse yet, if the services elect to continue on the current course, you may end up with a low-end MS-65 dollar that looks exactly like many of the other dollars in MS-64 holders. So either way you end up spending thousands of dollars for a coin that should be worth only a fraction of that.

Until and unless the grading services establish greater consistency in Peace dollars' grading, you would be well advised not to spend big bucks for a little bit higher grade.

GLOSSARY

People who buy and sell coins use many specific terms to describe them and talk about their production, condition, and value. Recognizing winners and losers in the coin market will be a great deal easier if you understand the meaning of these terms.

ask—the prices dealers are charging for particular coins.

bid—the "wholesale" prices dealers are offering to pay for certain coins.

Bluesheet—a descriptive term for the *Certified Coin Dealer Newsletter* (CCDN), a weekly guide that reports on the "sight-unseen" market for coins certified by grading services.

branch mint—a coin-making U.S. Mint facility other than the main mint in Philadelphia.

brilliant—a descriptive term for the bright, untoned surfaces of certain U.S. coins, especially proofs.

bullion—precious metal in bulk form, such as an ingot or bar.

business strike—a coin produced by the Mint for use in commerce.

cameo—a term describing the contrast between frosted fields (or background areas) and reflective devices (or raised areas) on a coin.

certified—a term applied to coins evaluated, authenticated, and encapsulated in hard, sonically sealed plastic holders by grading services.

Choice—a term for a mint state coin that is in better-than-average condition but less than "Gem."

circulated—a term for a coin that has been passed from hand to hand and bears evidence of wear from such use.

commemoratives—special coins issued to honor worthy persons or mark important events.

condition-census—the highest condition in which a coin exists (not the finest condition ever known or the finest condition possible).

consignor—a person who submits coins for an auction company to sell.

denomination—a coin's face value, such as cent, nickel, or dime.

devices—the raised parts of a coin, such as the lettering, portrait, and stars. On coins with incuse designs, the devices are below the surface.

die—a piece of steel bearing a design, used to stamp coins with that image.

DMPL—an abbreviation for Deep-Mirror Prooflike, a term used in grading coins, especially silver dollars, with exceptionally brilliant, reflective surfaces.

edge—the side of a coin.

fields—the parts of a coin that serve as background and don't stand out.

Gem—a term for a mint state coin of unusually high quality.

grade—the rating collectors use to describe a coin's level of preservation and overall attractiveness. Standard grading today uses a numerical system from 1 (barely recognizable) to 70 (flawless).

Greysheet—a descriptive term for the *Coin Dealer Newsletter* (*CDN*), a weekly publication widely used by dealers and collectors, and the *CDN Monthly Supplement*, an expanded publication issued monthly by the *CDN*.

hairlines—patches of light, almost imperceptible scratches, especially on proof coins, usually caused by cleaning.

impaired proof—a proof that has been mishandled, making its grade equivalent to that of a circulated business-strike coin.

lettered edge—a term used when a coin has an inscription on the side.

matte proof—a proof made by a process that creates dull, granular surfaces, sometimes described as having a "sandblast" appearance.

mintage—the number of examples of a specific coin produced with the same date at the same mint.

mint error—a coin with a mistake that occurred during its production, such as doubling of the date and off-center striking.

mint mark—the letter or letters on a coin denoting where it was made. Many coins from the Philadelphia Mint carried no mint mark in the past, but most now have a small "P." Similarly, coins struck at West Point either bear a "W" or have no mint mark. Other mint marks: S—San Francisco, D—Denver or (on pre-1862 gold coins) Dahlonega, O—New Orleans, CC—Carson City, C—Charlotte.

Mint State—the condition of a coin that has never seen use in circulation. Mint State coins should show no wear. "Mint State" and "uncirculated" are synonymous.

motto—an inscription, or legend, on a coin. Common mottos on U.S. coins include "Liberty," "In God We Trust," and "E Pluribus Unum."

NGC—the Numismatic Guaranty Corporation of America, one of the principal third-party coin-grading services.

numismatics—the study of coins, paper money, medals, tokens, and related items.

obverse—the "heads" side of a coin.

pattern—a test coin made by the Mint to see if an experimental metal or design is suitable for regular coinage.

PCGS—the Professional Coin Grading Service, the first and largest coin-grading service.

plain edge—a term for a coin whose side is smooth, not reeded or lettered.

planchet—a blank piece of metal ready to receive impressions from two dies and become a coin.

premium—the extra amount of money above face value that a coin is worth as a collector's item.

premium-quality (PQ)—a term applied to a coin of unusually high quality for its grade, which nearly qualifies for the next-highest grade.

proof—a coin struck multiple times for collectors on a flawless planchet, with specially polished dies, to impart a chromium-like brilliance.

prooflike (or PL)—a term used to describe a business-strike coin whose brilliant, reflective surfaces look like those of a proof.

Red Book—*A Guide Book of United States Coins*, by Richard S. Yeoman.

reeded edge—a term used when the side of a coin has sharp, regular ridges. These were placed initially on gold and silver coins to discourage removal of metal and remain in use today on many coins, even when they contain no precious metal.

registry set—a set of certified coins, typically in very high grades, assembled for inclusion in the Set Registry program of the Professional Coin Grading Service or a similar program of another grading service.

restrike—a genuine coin struck by the Mint years later with dies that suggest the coin was struck at an earlier date.

reverse—the "tails" side of a coin.

rims—the raised rings encircling the obverse and reverse of a coin and protecting it from wear.

slab—the hard plastic, tamper-resistant holder in which a coin is sealed by a grading service.

slider—a coin that is only slightly worn and appears to be uncirculated.

state quarter—a special quarter dollar issued by the U.S. Mint as part of its 50-State Quarters Program. Each quarter in this series, which started in 1999, bears a commemorative design honoring one of the 50 states of the Union.

strike—the degree of design detail present on a coin at the time it is minted.

toning—the slow, natural process by which a coin oxidizes over a period of months and years. Tarnish, by contrast, is quick and unnatural.

type—a major coin design, such as the Lincoln cent or Jefferson nickel. This term is sometimes used to refer to a variety, as in "Type 1 Buffalo nickel." Varieties are actually coins of the same type which differ in one or more significant details.

uncirculated—a term applied to a coin that has never been spent or seen any other circulation. Such a coin should have no wear on its highest parts.

wear—the erosion of a coin's top layer of metal that results from use in circulation.

ABOUT THE AUTHOR

Scott A. Travers ranks as one of the most knowledgeable and influential coin dealers in the world. His name is familiar to readers everywhere as the author of seven best-selling books on coins: *The Coin Collector's Survival Manual*®, *One-Minute Coin Expert*®, *How to Make Money in Coins Right Now*, *Travers' Rare Coin Investment Strategy*, *Scott Travers' Top 88 to Buy & Sell*, *The Insider's Guide to U.S. Coin Values*, and *The Investor's Guide to Coin Trading*. All of them have won awards from the prestigious Numismatic Literary Guild (NLG). In 2002, NLG awarded him its highest honor, the lifetime achievement Clemy. He was elected vice president (1997–99) of the American Numismatic Association, a congressionally chartered, nonprofit educational organization. He is a contributing editor to *COINage* magazine and a regular contributor to other numismatic periodicals, and has served as a coin valuation consultant to the Federal Trade Commission. His opinions as an expert are often sought by publications such as *Barron's*, *Business Week*, and the *Wall Street Journal*. A frequent guest on radio and television programs from the *Today Show* to *Inside Edition*, Scott Travers has won awards and gained an impressive reputation not only as a coin expert but also as a forceful consumer advocate for the coin-buying public. He serves as numismatic adviser to a number of major investment funds and has coordinated the liquidation of numerous important coin collections. He is president and member of Scott Travers Rare Coin Galleries, LLC, in New York City.

CONTACT THE AUTHOR

The author welcomes your comments and reports of your winners and losers. Every inquiry will be carefully studied.

Scott A. Travers

Scott Travers Rare Coin Galleries, LLC

P.O. Box 1711

F.D.R. Station

New York, NY 10150-1711

Telephone: 212-535-9135

E-mail: travers@PocketChangeLottery.com

Internet: www.PocketChangeLottery.com